How to
Write Off Your
Down Payment

How to Write Off Your Down Payment

Nelson E. Brestoff

G. P. Putnam's Sons
New York

G. P. Putnam's Sons
Publishers Since 1838
200 Madison Avenue
New York, NY 10016

This publication is designed to provide accurate and authoritative information in regard to the subject matter covered. It is sold with the understanding that the publisher is not engaged in rendering legal, accounting, or other professional service. If legal advice or other expert assistance is required, the services of a competent professional person should be sought.

From a "Declaration of Principles jointly adopted by a Committee of the American Bar Association and a Committee of Publishers."

Library of Congress Cataloging-in-Publication Data

Brestoff, Nelson E.
  How to write off your down payment.

  Bibliography: p.
  Includes index.
  1. Depreciation allowances—Law and legislation—
United States. 2. Vendors and purchasers—Taxation—
United States. I. Title.
KF6386.B74 1985   343.7305'46   85-19108
ISBN 0-399-13058-6   347.303546

Acknowledgments

In *How to Borrow Money Below Prime* (Simon and Schuster, 1985), I acknowledged the engineering and science professors who taught me how to think analytically. I also thanked the bankers who allowed me to see how they calculate the profitability of a customer's relationship. In this book, I must acknowledge a few lawyers.

Samuel K. Freshman is a legend in the real estate business, first as a lawyer and then as the president of a syndication and property management company. He wrote *Principles of Real Estate Syndication* in 1973 and, for a generation, has shown the way as a real estate deal maker. He was writing about "soft dollars" (a phrase that is very important to this book) long before me. Sam has been right so often that he's one of the rare lawyers who can give advice to himself. I greatly appreciate his comments and corrections to the manuscript.

John A. Barclay, of Newport Beach, California, is still my partner in several real estate ventures. Although we no longer practice law together, we have remained good friends. A great deal of the insight that you'll find in this book was born in the way John handled deals for our clients. Chapter 10 is based on his draft.

George Wall and Robert Jay Grossman practice law in Newport Beach and Los Angeles, California, respectively, and specialize in tax and securities matters. George reviewed an early draft and Bob edited the page proofs, and I am grateful for their keen eyes and helpful comments. They assure me that my readers will have a much easier time communicating with their tax advisors, be they lawyers or accountants.

Finally, Lois M. Brestoff deserves special recognition for the tax research you'll find as notes to various chapters.

Regardless of all these fine contributions, of course, the responsibility for the material is mine alone, fair weather or foul.

To my wife, Lois, our sons, Daniel and Jonathan,
my brother, Richard,
my mother, Dee Parker Brestoff Cherney,
my stepfather, Guy Cherney,
and in memory of my father, Phillip F. Brestoff.

Contents

Chief Seattle's Message

(This address was given on the occasion of the transfer of the ancestral lands of the Suquamish Indians in Washington Territory to the United States. Before we get into the brainwork in this book, I offer Chief Seattle's message in the same vein as prayer. Before we nourish our bodies, we should nourish our souls.)

The Great Chief in Washington sends word that he wishes to buy our land.

The Great Chief also sends us words of friendship and good will. This is kind of him, since we know he has little need of our friendship in return. But we will consider your offer. For we know that if we do not sell, the white man may come with guns and take our land.

How can you buy or sell the sky, the warmth of the land? The idea is strange to us.

If we do not own the freshness of the air and the sparkle of the water, how can you buy them?

Every part of this earth is sacred to my people. Every shining pine needle, every sandy shore, every mist in the dark woods, every clearing and humming insect is holy in the memory and experience of my people. The sap which courses through the trees carries the memories of the red man.

The white man's dead forget the country of their birth when they go to walk among the stars. Our dead never forget this beautiful earth, for it is the mother of the red man. We are part of the earth and it is part of us. The perfumed flowers are our sisters; the deer, the horse, the great eagle, these are our brothers. The rocky crests, the juices in the meadows, the body heat of the pony, and man—all belong to the same family. . . .

This shining water that moves in the streams and rivers is not just water but the blood of our ancestors. If we sell you land, you must remember that it is sacred, and you must teach your children that it is sacred, and that each ghostly reflection in the clear water of the lake tells of events and memories in the life of my people. The water's murmur is the voice of my father's father.

The rivers are our brothers, they quench our thirst. The rivers carry our canoes, and feed our children. If we sell you our land, you must remember, and teach your children, that the rivers are our brothers, and yours, and you must henceforth give the rivers the kindness you would give any brother.

The red man has always retreated before the advancing white man, as the mist of the mountains runs before the morning sun. But the ashes of our fathers are sacred. Their graves are holy ground, and so these hills, these trees, this portion of earth is consecrated to us. We know that the white man does not understand our ways. One portion of land is the same to him as the next, for he is a stranger who comes in the night and takes from the land whatever he needs. The earth is not his brother, but his enemy, and when he has conquered it, he moves on. He leaves his fathers' graves behind, and he does not care. He kidnaps the earth from his children. He does not care. His fathers' graves and his children's birthright are forgotten. He treats his mother, the earth, and his brother, the sky, as things to be bought, plundered, sold like sheep or bright beads. His appetite will devour the earth and leave behind only a desert. . . .

The air is precious to the red man, for all things share the same breath—the beast, the tree, the man, they all share the same breath. . . . The wind that gave our grandfather his first breath also receives his last sigh. And the wind must also give our children the spirit of life. . . .

What is man without the beasts? If all the beasts were gone, men would die from a great loneliness of spirit. For whatever happens to the beasts, soon happens to man. All things are connected.

You must teach your children that the ground beneath their feet is the ashes of our grandfathers. So that they will respect the land, tell your children that the earth is rich with the lives of our kin. Teach your children what we have taught our children, that the earth is our mother. Whatever befalls the earth, befalls the sons of the earth. If men spit upon the ground they spit upon themselves.

This we know. The earth does not belong to man; man belongs to the earth. This we know. All things are connected like the blood which unites one family. All things are connected.

Whatever befalls the earth befalls the sons of the earth. Man did not weave the web of life; he is merely a strand in it. Whatever he does to the web, he does to himself. . . .

Even the white man, whose God walks and talks with him as friend to friend, cannot be exempt from the common destiny. We may be brothers after all; we shall see. One thing we know, which the white man may one day discover—our God is the same God. You may think now that you own him as you wish to own our land; but you cannot. He is the God of man, and his compassion is equal for the red man and the white. This earth is precious to him, and to harm the earth is to heap contempt on its Creator. . . . So if we sell you our land, love it as we've loved it. Care for it as we've cared for it. Hold in your mind the memory of the land as it is when you take it. And with all your strength, with all your mind, with all your heart, preserve it for your children, and love it . . . as God loves us all. . . .

Foreword

The road to riches has very few signposts marked "nothing down." While it is worthwhile to try the "nothing down" approach, a buyer usually finds that some down payment is required.

My basic acquisition philosophy is that the eventual profit is determined by how well something is bought. Indeed, there is a business maxim that "well bought is half sold." Buying more often than not involves a down payment, the key factor to a good purchase. By learning how to structure a deal to minimize the impact of a down payment when it can't be avoided, you'll learn in this book how to turn the typical 20 percent to 30 percent cash down payment deal into that "nothing down" deal that you've been searching for.

For most people, the most crucial variables in any deal are the terms of the financing—the maturity date and interest rates—and the size of the down payment.

In *How to Borrow Money Below Prime* (Simon and Schuster, 1985), Nelson E. Brestoff (Nick to his friends) focused on the problem of high interest rates. He explained how to negotiate for bank loans at rates far less than the vast majority of people and businesses were paying. He showed how to get a competitive edge by reducing the cost of bank debt, and how to overcome a general naiveté concerning interest rates.

This book is about another problem: how to handle a down payment when you have to make one.

In this book, Nick explains how to handle real estate and business deals when a down payment *is* required. He shows how to turn what would otherwise be "iceberg" equity (which he explains in the first chapter) into tax writeoffs. These dollars, which would otherwise go for the down payment, are converted from iceberg equity into tax writeoffs. In the highest and most sophisticated levels of big-time real estate syndication deals, these are called "soft dollars."

Nick brings this all down to earth.

Real estate investment professionals know what "soft dollars" are and use the phrase all the time. I am not, of course, talking about the role of the dollar in the international marketplace. Nor does Nick discuss the strength or weakness of the dollar versus the Japanese yen or the German mark. Nor are we talking about "soft costs," the phrase used in the construction business to cover architectural, engineering, and other professional fees that are incurred before a spadeful of dirt is turned. Finally, this book has nothing whatever to do with "soft dollars" as the phrase is sometimes used on Wall Street. There, when a trader pays for brokerage commissions with the research thrown in free, the arrangement is a "soft dollar" deal. Nick won't be dealing with this at all.

What Nick does cover, however, is how to convert those down payment dollars from being non-expensable, out-of-pocket, and hard-to-part-with into writeoffs that will boost your yield. With the soft dollar technique at your fingertips, you can turn poor deals into acceptable ones and acceptable deals into exceptional ones.

Stay with it even if the sledding gets rough. This is sophisticated stuff, made simple.

One final thought. I'm well aware that Congress is debating a number of tax reforms. This book isn't a treatise on the existing rules, or a history of the changes in the rules over the years. It is a book about how to make deals.

SAMUEL K. FRESHMAN
Chairman and President
Standard Management Company
Los Angeles, California

Introduction

Crafty men condemn studies; simple men admire them;
and wise men use them.
—Sir Francis Bacon

Almost every real estate deal involves tax planning. Tax planning isn't tax evasion, it's a necessity, and all of us are entitled to plan our affairs in ways that minimize Uncle Sam's long-arm reach into our lives.

I don't want to be cavalier about this, however. The distinction between tax planning and tax evasion is twofold. Planning is allowed. Cheating is not. That's the first distinction. The second distinction is that planning takes awareness and creativity. Cheating is the easy way into a lot of trouble.

The deal presented by the seller is probably *not* the best deal for the buyer from a tax point of view. The problem, then, is to know enough about the basic rules to visualize alternatives that haven't been considered. Such alternatives often involve a reconsideration (during negotiations) of the deal, and sometimes call for a completely different form of transaction. When another road is taken, the documentation will be completely different.

Tax planning also involves a kind of double-track process. This will be especially clear in Chapter 3 ("Two, Two, Two Deals in One"). This is possibility thinking applied to real estate and business deal-making.

My principal aim here is to impart the basic notions of tax planning so that you can see more possibilities and make more and better deals. Please know that I am writing as a businessman and real estate lawyer, not as a tax attorney. Because our tax laws are ultradynamic these days, it is not my purpose to teach the rules of the Internal Revenue Code. Tax lawyers chart these shifting sands of laws, regulations, and rulings. I spend my time making deals and writing books (when I'm not in court).

My goal is to impart some of the wisdom I've culled from experience. In order to put my main point across, however, I'm forced to skip a great many fine points. This isn't a treatise; it's a tour through the mind of a lawyer who plays with tax laws as if they were merely verbal formulae to be pushed around. After explaining the basics of the rules, I show how they interact with one another and with the deal points I'm considering.

But since I can't foresee how the laws will apply to your particular situation, I urge you to consult your advisors *before* you sign the contract, not afterward. Planning takes place during negotiations, not after the contract is signed. If, after you have read this book, you ask better questions or conceive more creative approaches to the deal, then I'll have done my job.

The "wisdom" of this book has nothing to to with the law as it stands today. I've lived through a number of major changes in the tax laws in the last few years, and no doubt there are more changes yet to come. The most important thing this book will do is teach you to use the kind of thinking *behind* the techniques that I'll explain. If you'll read the book at that level, you'll learn how to deal the cards correctly no matter how often Congress shuffles the deck.

More than anything else, this will require you to have an open mind, to be intellectually curious. Though you may not yet have found lawyers who are "possibility thinkers," this book is more about such "possibility thinking" than anything else.

Oh, by the way, the title is a bit misleading. You can't, strictly speaking, write off your down payment. But in a way reminiscent of a magician's sleight of hand, I will show you how to write off what you used to think of as the down payment (by "write off" I mean expensing or amortizing of costs incurred).

Your first clue: if you can't write off your down payment, don't make one.

1

Iceberg Equity

As a real estate lawyer and investor, I have a view of equity different from that of many people who lived through the Depression. Some of the people who lived through those hard times are understandably fearful of debt. They want to own their homes free and clear. It used to be cause for celebration when the debt was paid off and it was time to "burn the mortgage."

Today, more than fifty years since the terrible times of 1933, the wounds are in the distant past and their sting has been forgotten. This doesn't mean that we're destined to repeat our mistakes. Rather, I think, we're far enough away from the calamities of the thirties that they no longer fog our vision.

Let's look at a few examples of the meaning of "equity." When I'm through you'll see that equity can be a losing proposition. Assuming some degree of inflation, equity is like banking your money in a *negative*-interest account.

In a hypothetical example, which I'll be using throughout the book, we'll buy a $100,000 duplex. Our goal is to hold it for investment purposes in an environment of 5 percent inflation. Under the terms of our purchase, completed on January 1 of our hypothetical year, we're going to make a heavy down payment of $50,000, or 50 percent of the purchase price. This will leave a $50,000 balance, which, at 12 percent interest, will cost $500 per month in interest-only payments. Let's assume we can rent out our duplex for a total of $800 per month ($400 for each unit), and during the year, spend $1,100 for property taxes, $1,000 for maintenance, $900 for utilities, and $600 for miscellaneous items. The total, $3,600, is roughly 35 percent of gross income. This is a fairly typical percentage for operational expenses before debt service (new buildings are lower; older buildings can be higher). At the end of the year, our cash flow will be, again roughly, zero (see Figure 1-1).

Zero? If we're making an *investment*, why would we go ahead if our cash flow were going to be zero?

The answer, of course, is twofold: the opportunity for future appreciation and the reality of a present tax break.

The tax break is depreciation. Under the tax rules for ownership of business or investment property, the portion of the value of the property attributed to the structure (land never depreciates) can be evenly depreciated over eighteen years or at an even faster rate in the early years using "accelerated depreciation" (which I'll explain in Chapters 5 and 6).

In our hypothetical case, let's assume that the tax assessor's records show that $72,000 of the duplex's value is attributable to the structure. The land value is $28,000. If we use straight-line depreciation (equal writeoffs in each of the eighteen years), we can write off $4,000 each year.

Since all of our monthly $500 payment goes to pay interest, which is a currently deductible expense, our profit-and-loss ("P&L") statement for the year gives us our tax position (see Figure 1-1).

What I've contrived here is the classic tax shelter. From a cash flow point of view, the property's operation is only break-even. From a tax point of view, however, we have a loss. (By the way, when bankers analyze your tax return or financial statement, they add depreciation back to the profit or loss to see how you're doing from a cash flow point of view.)

This tax loss may not look like a tangible benefit, but it is, because the loss can be used to offset other income (say, from a salary) for tax purposes. It's this aspect of the investment that gives the tax "shelter" its name. The noncash loss shelters the cash-in-hand income. Income from services rendered is usually sheltered from tax with a tax loss investment based on depreciation writeoffs. Real losses aren't any good to anyone.

Before we get back to discussing equity, let's put a value on the tax "benefit" that attracted us to this wonderful investment opportunity in the first place. In order to arrive at the *value* of the tax loss ($4,000), we have to prepare two hypothetical tax returns, one with the benefits, one without.

CASH FLOW

Income		$ 9,600
Expenses		
1. Interest	$6,000	
2. Property Taxes	1,100	
3. Maintenance	1,000	
4. Utilities	900	
5. Miscellaneous	600	
Total Expenses		$ 9,600
Net Cash		$ –0–

TAX POSITION

Income ($800 × 12)		$ 9,600
Expenses		
1. Interest ($500 × 12)	$6,000	
2. Property Taxes	1,100	
3. Maintenance	1,000	
4. Utilities	900	
5. Miscellaneous	600	
6. Depreciation	4,000	
Total Expenses		$13,600
Net Profit (Loss)		($ 4,000)

Figure 1-1. Hypothetical Cash Flow and Tax Position for $100,000 Duplex.

In the first case, let's assume that we didn't buy the duplex, didn't spend our $50,000, and have no tax loss like this at all. We still have our $50,000. Does it help us reduce our taxes? No, because, if anything, we probably earned interest income on the money and added that to our other income already subject to tax. Let's suppose that you and your spouse earned salaries totaling $35,000, earned $5,000 in interest ($50,000 × 10 percent) and had a short-term loss in the stock market of $11,600. Your taxable net income is $28,400 ($35,000 + $5,000 − $11,600). So, $28,400 is what will show up on your friendly Form 1040 as the amount subject to tax.

If you use Tax Rate Schedule Y (Figure 1-2), married filing a joint return, you'll see that the tax is $3,465 plus 25 percent of

Figure 1-2.

1984 Tax Rate Schedules
Your zero bracket amount has been built into these Tax Rate Schedules.

Caution: You must use the Tax Table instead of these Tax Rate Schedules if your taxable income is less than $50,000 unless you use **Schedule G**, Income Averaging, to figure your tax. In that case, even if your taxable income is less than $50,000, use the rate schedules on this page to figure your tax.

Schedule X
Single Taxpayers

Use this Schedule if you checked **Filing Status Box 1** on Form 1040—

If the amount on Form 1040, line 37 is: Over—	But not over—	Enter on Form 1040, line 38	of the amount over—
$0	$2,300	—0—	
2,300	3,400	......11%	$2,300
3,400	4,400	$121 + 12%	3,400
4,400	6,500	241 + 14%	4,400
6,500	8,500	535 + 15%	6,500
8,500	10,800	835 + 16%	8,500
10,800	12,900	1,203 + 18%	10,800
12,900	15,000	1,581 + 20%	12,900
15,000	18,200	2,001 + 23%	15,000
18,200	23,500	2,737 + 26%	18,200
23,500	28,800	4,115 + 30%	23,500
28,800	34,100	5,705 + 34%	28,800
34,100	41,500	7,507 + 38%	34,100
41,500	55,300	10,319 + 42%	41,500
55,300	81,800	16,115 + 48%	55,300
81,800	....	28,835 + 50%	81,800

Schedule Z
Unmarried Heads of Household
(including certain married persons who live apart—see page 5 of the instructions)

Use this schedule if you checked **Filing Status Box 4** on Form 1040—

If the amount on Form 1040, line 37 is: Over—	But not over—	Enter on Form 1040, line 38	of the amount over—
$0	$2,300	—0—	
2,300	4,400	......11%	$2,300
4,400	6,500	$231 + 12%	4,400
6,500	8,700	483 + 14%	6,500
8,700	11,800	791 + 17%	8,700
11,800	15,000	1,318 + 18%	11,800
15,000	18,200	1,894 + 20%	15,000
18,200	23,500	2,534 + 24%	18,200
23,500	28,800	3,806 + 28%	23,500
28,800	34,100	5,290 + 32%	28,800
34,100	44,700	6,986 + 35%	34,100
44,700	60,600	10,696 + 42%	44,700
60,600	81,800	17,374 + 45%	60,600
81,800	108,300	26,914 + 48%	81,800
108,300	....	39,634 + 50%	108,300

Schedule Y
Married Taxpayers and Qualifying Widows and Widowers

Married Filing Joint Returns and Qualifying Widows and Widowers

Use this schedule if you checked **Filing Status Box 2 or 5** on Form 1040—

If the amount on Form 1040, line 37 is: Over—	But not over—	Enter on Form 1040, line 38	of the amount over—
$0	$3,400	—0—	
3,400	5,500	......11%	$3,400
5,500	7,600	$231 + 12%	5,500
7,600	11,900	483 + 14%	7,600
11,900	16,000	1,085 + 16%	11,900
16,000	20,200	1,741 + 18%	16,000
20,200	24,600	2,497 + 22%	20,200
24,600	29,900	3,465 + 25%	24,600
29,900	35,200	4,790 + 28%	29,900
35,200	45,800	6,274 + 33%	35,200
45,800	60,000	9,772 + 38%	45,800
60,000	85,600	15,168 + 42%	60,000
85,600	109,400	25,920 + 45%	85,600
109,400	162,400	36,630 + 49%	109,400
162,400	....	62,600 + 50%	162,400

Married Filing Separate Returns

Use this schedule if you checked **Filing Status Box 3** on Form 1040—

If the amount on Form 1040, line 37 is: Over—	But not over—	Enter on Form 1040, line 38	of the amount over—
$0	$1,700	—0—	
1,700	2,750	......11%	$1,700
2,750	3,800	$115.50 + 12%	2,750
3,800	5,950	241.50 + 14%	3,800
5,950	8,000	542.50 + 16%	5,950
8,000	10,100	870.50 + 18%	8,000
10,100	12,300	1,248.50 + 22%	10,100
12,300	14,950	1,732.50 + 25%	12,300
14,950	17,600	2,395.00 + 28%	14,950
17,600	22,900	3,137.00 + 33%	17,600
22,900	30,000	4,886.00 + 38%	22,900
30,000	42,800	7,584.00 + 42%	30,000
42,800	54,700	12,960.00 + 45%	42,800
54,700	81,200	18,315.00 + 49%	54,700
81,200	....	31,300.00 + 50%	81,200

the amount over $24,600. Since the "amount over" is $3,800, the additional tax is $950 ($3,800 × 25 percent) and the total is $4,415 ($3,465 + $950). The first figure in the third column of Schedule Y is your base tax ($3,465). The second figure is your bracket rate (25 percent). In effect, the bracket rate means that for every dollar of net income over $24,600, 25 percent will be lost to taxes.

The highest federal bracket rate for 1984 was 50 percent, beginning at $81,800 for single taxpayers, and $162,400 for husband and wife filing a joint return. In other words, after you get to these levels, you have to make two dollars to keep one. You have an *equal partner* in Uncle Sam for every *extra* dollar of net income earned after $81,800 if you're single and for every dollar of net income earned after $162,400 if you're married. (In some states, of course, there is a state income tax. In other states, like Texas, there is none. For ease of illustration, I'm going to assume we're in Texas and ignore state income taxes.)

If business weren't such fun, most of us would quit at these levels. When we go beyond them, and do all the work for half the reward, it can only be because the intangible fun outweighs both the risk and the emotional wear and tear.

Now that we've got one tax return completed, let's factor in our tax shelter. We've spent our $50,000 and forgone our $5,000 in interest income. We still have our $35,000 salary and our stock loss of $11,600. With our tax shelter loss of $4,000, however, our net taxable income drops to $19,400 ($35,000 − $11,600 − $4,000). According to Schedule Y (married filing a joint return), we're in the 18 percent tax bracket. The tax is $1,741 plus 18 percent of every net taxable dollar over $16,000 ($19,400 − $16,000 = $3,400 × 18 percent = $612). Our total tax would be $2,353 ($1,741 + $612).

To summarize, the tax without our shelter is $4,415. The tax *with* our shelter is $2,353. We saved $2,062. But since we gave up $5,000 in interest income, we're really $2,938 behind. This is the price we're paying for the opportunity of acquiring a duplex that may appreciate more rapidly than that humdrum interest-bearing account.

As you can see, our tax saving ($2,062) is 52 percent of our

$4,000 tax shelter. The shelter is not effective for us on a dollar-for-dollar basis. Tax losses are only valuable to the extent we can reduce our taxes. The rest is wasted.

Realistically, all things are not equal. When you choose between alternatives, you might be giving up an income opportunity like the $5,000 in interest income in our hypothetical example; income that would, of course, be taxed. While the bracket rates are a good indication of the effect of any particular course of action, you can determine the effect in precise terms only by completing two different returns—one with the shelter and one without it.

This is different from the way tax losses are estimated by tax shelter offerings. People who devise tax shelter programs usually show two bracket calculations: 50 percent and 30 percent. What they're saying is that the value to a 50 percent bracket taxpayer is fifty cents for every dollar in estimated net tax losses. This assumes that the taxpayer will be in the 50 percent bracket both before and after the shelter is applied. Similarly, the value for someone in the 30 percent bracket is presumably thirty cents for every dollar in estimated tax losses.

As you can see from our hypothetical example, this isn't strictly true. In our example, we dropped from the 25 percent bracket into the 18 percent bracket, but we saved almost half of our tax bill.

But tax brackets *are* important in a sophisticated way. Tax rates and bracket calculations are ways of analyzing the impact of events "at the margin." This "marginal" thinking is a very useful, very powerful conceptual aid to understanding finance (and many other things). When economists or mathematicians talk about "marginal" growth, they're looking at the impact of what just happened. It's a process of continuously taking one's pulse and asking about the impact of any change. The questions are always focused on *now*. The past is irrelevant.

Let's take a few examples. Let's focus on the 50 percent bracket for a moment. For each dollar earned over $81,800 for a single person ($162,400 for a married couple filing a joint return), we now know what will happen. We'll send 50 percent to Uncle Sam. There's no higher bracket. What happens to the 162,401st dollar is the same thing that happens to the 200,000th dollar—half of it is taxed away.

For a lower bracket, the story is more dynamic. In the 25 percent bracket, what happens to the 24,601st dollar is the same thing that happens to the 29,899th dollar: 25 percent of each additional dollar is taxed away. When we reach the 29,900th dollar, however, something new happens. The bracket rate, or marginal rate, *increases*. For every dollar of additional income over $29,900, 28 percent is taxed away. The marginal rate structure of our tax system is such that taxes grow at an increasingly faster clip until the point at which Uncle Sam takes half of whatever you've managed to net (and it was 70 percent until 1982).

This is the kind of thinking that helps you decide whether that additional dollar of income is worth the risk. And in asking that question, note that it is completely pointless to worry about the previous dollars earned. Each dollar called for the same decision, but the decision applied only to that dollar. The first dollar of income was taxed so lightly that you went on (and besides, you needed the money). When you got to the 20,000th dollar, did it matter what the decision had been regarding dollar one? No. The past is irrelevant. The only question is whether the *next* dollar is worth having.

This is so important that it's worth going through again with another example. This time, let's get away from money. Instead of money, let's talk about the weather. For this example, we'll imagine ourselves standing on the sea-level portion of an iceberg floating in the Atlantic during a snowstorm. For each snowflake that falls, of course, the iceberg gets a little bit heavier. After hours of snowfall, of course, the iceberg will only grow by a *fraction* of the snow that's fallen on it. Some of it went underwater. In fact, approximately 90 percent of an iceberg is underwater. Roughly 10 percent stays on top. After our snowfall, this will still be true, because the relative densities of the ice and the surrounding water generate a relatively constant rate of underwater growth. For every pound of snowflakes that falls, roughly 10 percent stays on top; 90 percent goes underwater. The same thing happens to each additional snowflake, and it doesn't matter how much of the iceberg is already underwater. We're still only comparing the density of those *additional* snowflakes relative to that of the surrounding water.

Now, we *could* look at it in two ways, considering either the growth at the top (at the margin) or the growth underwater—but we'd make a conceptual mistake if we did. The only relevant activity is the *growth-generating* activity—the falling snowflakes. Only the growth "at the margin" makes any difference. That's where the snowfall takes place. The portion that goes underwater depends only on the relative densities of water and ice, something that never changes.

Once a snowflake goes underwater, it, like our equity, is frozen. Although it is added to all those other crystals of frozen equity, none of them are growing either.

This example unmasks an important lesson: *Equity doesn't grow.* Equity can be increased, of course. Icebergs—including the underwater portions—do get larger. But our duplex would increase in value "at the margin" (because of inflation, for example) if there were $2 in equity (heavy debt), just as it would if there were $99,998 in equity (nearly zero debt). Neither equity nor debt per se have any impact on value or the rate of growth.

Equity, therefore, doesn't grow. Equity is underwater. If there's no snow (that is, if there's no inflation or market appreciation), there's no upside. Growth takes place "at the margin" and completely independent of whatever equity, or debt, there might be.

In fact (and there's a long breath needed here before we go on), our equity is *losing* value. Quantitatively, each unit of equity (in dollars or snowflakes) is the same size as when it was created. Equity does not bear children. It is rock solid, except for real depreciation (that is, obsolescence). Whether it's withdrawn after one year or after ten it's still the same amount.

But time marches on, and time has a monetary value—interest. Our equity doesn't earn this time value and therefore has relatively *less* purchasing power (assuming any positive rate of inflation) when withdrawn—compared, that is, to dollars that *have* earned interest equal to the rate of inflation.

Thus, if there's inflation, frozen equity dollars lose value. Always. They never have an opportunity to appreciate by participating in the marketplace or to earn interest. They are declining in value at the rate of interest that they would have earned, but didn't. This lost opportunity is known as an opportunity cost—the cost of missing out on the opportunity to earn interest.

This "missed opportunity" cost is a slippery concept, because nothing appears to have changed. Although the amount of our frozen equity doesn't grow, it doesn't appear to shrink either. Since we are continually forced to choose between alternatives, opportunity costs are unavoidable. For example, if we switched our equity out of real estate and into cash in order to earn interest, we'd be giving up the opportunity to take advantage of tax incentives like depreciation and the opportunity for appreciation in our real estate portfolio. Since these opportunity costs are behind every bush, I treat them like a fixed and benign piece of scenery. I also ignore them because I never know in advance whether one opportunity cost (forgone interest) will be greater or less than another (forgone shelter or forgone appreciation). Hindsight is accurate, but not helpful in deciding what to do. So much for the theoretical opportunity cost. For practical purposes, I just don't worry about it.

The practical matter that has just cropped up, however, is the transaction cost. In the last paragraph, I mentioned switching out of a real estate investment and into cash. This can cost around 8 percent of our selling price. If we get cash by selling our real estate, we might have to pay 6 percent to the broker(s); 1 percent to a good real estate lawyer (the deal maker kind), and another 1 percent in title insurance premiums and closing costs. If we get cash by borrowing from a third party and pledging our equity as collateral, we'll have cashed out our equity and incurred different kinds of charges: 1–3 "points" (one "point" is 1 percent of the loan amount; also called "origination fees" or "loan fees," points are paid to the lender at the time the loan is made), 1 percent in mortgage insurance premiums and closing costs, and a 1–4 percent differential between the interest we have to pay on the loan and the interest income we can earn on the loan proceeds.

For brokers, lawyers, and title insurance companies, a rapid succession of transactions (known as "churning") is a wonderful generator of fees. For sellers and buyers, who often share these costs in some way, these "transaction costs" are far more real than opportunity costs. In fact, because these fees are usually paid in cash, their significance is usually magnified by the fact that the amount of cash in the deal is only a fraction of the purchase price. If the fees payable in cash are 5 percent of our

$100,000 purchase price ($5,000), and if the cash down payment is a familiar 20 percent ($20,000), a 5 percent transaction cost adds up to *25 percent* of the cash involved.

This brings us to a discussion of leverage. Leverage, in the acquisition of real estate, is an extremely important feature. In a deal that is highly leveraged, the buyer has very little of his or her own cash invested as a down payment, the ultimate being a "nothing down" deal. A deal that is poorly leveraged might involve a 30 percent to 50 percent down payment. An all-cash deal is a deal with no leverage at all.

Let's suppose we wanted to buy a $1 million apartment complex with 10 percent down and a $900,000 note. If inflation (or market appreciation) were 5 percent per annum, the complex would be worth $1,050,000 in a `year and, by compounding, slightly more than $1,102,500 in two years. If we could cash out this increase and our equity, and simply pass along the $900,000 debt we acquired when we bought the place, we'd get back $202,500 on our initial $100,000 investment, a profit of $102,500 in two years. On an annualized yield basis (profit divided by investment), this is an average of 51.25 percent per year ($102,500 ÷ $100,000 = 102.5% ÷ 2 years), a yield which looks far more attractive than bank interest.

And note that the increase was "at the margin" and completely independent of how much equity was involved. Had there been $1 million in equity (or debt) the amount of appreciation ($102,500 in 2 years) would have been the same.

Contrast this result with that in a no-leverage situation. We'll buy the project for $1 million *all cash* and sell it for $1,102,500 all cash in the same two-year period. Our average annual yield here is only 5.125 percent ($102,500 ÷ $1,000,000 = 10.25% ÷ 2), a figure which is probably *less* than money market rates. We might have done better if we had avoided tying up our $1 million and instead invested the cash in a government instrument (a treasury bill) at a safe and modest rate of 8 to 12 percent per year.

This illustration allows me to make a concluding remark about equity. Note that our yield drops considerably when we're forced to commit a large fraction of the purchase price as equity. *The lower the equity, the less we have to lose (in terms of dollars out of our pocket) and the more we stand to gain in terms of yield.*

Since our hoped-for appreciation is a function of *market value* and *depends not at all on equity,* we'd all be better off structuring deals with "nothing down." There's no equity to lose if the deal goes sour; no equity frozen and going nowhere; no constraints on our cash available to make other deals; and no limit to our yield. For buyers who can handle negative cash flow, this is a winning strategy.

The world is, however, composed of both buyers and sellers. In every deal, there's one of each. Every buyer dreams of a "nothing down" deal. What do you suppose every seller wants?

Of course. All cash.

2
The Double-Edged Sword

Now that we've explored the topic of equity, we see that equity is, in itself, a dubious proposition—at least at the outset. A lot of equity, however, produces something else: *cash flow*. If we've sunk a fortune into our iceberg, then there's little or no debt to service with payments of principal and interest. After our operating expenses, the money that would otherwise go into debt service goes right to the bottom line. After you've built a lot of equity, it generates cash flow.

The "nothing down" approach is the "high leverage" gambit. This is where most of us begin. Since this approach involves a lot of debt, there's usually no cash flow. Indeed, real estate investments are often so highly leveraged that the high loan payments result in a *negative* cash flow. For properties that have no potential for immediate rehabilitation or upgrading of some kind, such loans are called "crocodile" loans. To keep a crocodile happy, you have to keep feeding it. Crocodiles tend to eat up not only all the cash the property can itself generate, but also their owner's pocketbook.

So, simply put, the extremes are shown below.

HIGH LEVERAGE	LOW LEVERAGE
• LOW EQUITY	• HIGH EQUITY
• NEGATIVE CASH FLOW	• POSITIVE CASH FLOW

In a nutshell, the only way around the low equity, negative cash flow dilemma is to find a seller who's so desperate that he or she will sell for no cash and walk away from whatever equity he or she once may have had. The buyer inherits the existing loans. Assuming continued inflation (a very important assumption) and a lot of "sweat equity," this approach may net a profit, providing that you can hold on to that crocodile long enough. Stay with that crocodile (that is, pay the price along the way by feeding the negative cash flow) and inflation may turn you into a genius.

Suppose you've built up a portfolio of twenty houses over a ten-year period. With leverage, you can control a great deal of real estate with very little money. If you can hang on, you might decide to sell half of your portfolio, the half bought during the early years, on which inflation has had the most effect. With the profits, you might pay down the mortgages on the rest of the portfolio. This would create cash flow and an "easy street" life.

However, this is easier said than done. Building up that portfolio of twenty houses with a high leverage, nothing down strategy is no simple task. One key reason for the practical difficulty is that leverage is a double-edged sword. If you're highly leveraged, then you're only one step ahead of that greedy crocodile and, perhaps, a petition in bankruptcy.

With real estate, however, it's sometimes possible to make a mistake without paying too dearly for it. For example, if you buy a piece of property for "nothing down," then you've got no equity to lose in the event of a foreclosure. This only applies, however, when the lenders can't go after the buyer for any deficiency (that is, any shortfall on their loan after the sale of the property). They can only foreclose and take the property themselves. It's their only collateral. In California, lenders and sellers who make loans in connection with the sale of real estate (known as a purchase money mortgage) have no right to go after a buyer for any deficiency that might result if the property, when sold, fails to bring enough to cover their "purchase money" loan. In other words, the lenders can do nothing more than take the property back, as "real estate owned," or REO property.

This regulation doesn't apply in most states or in all situations. For example, in California, a deficiency judgment is possible when the loan is a "hard money" loan, a loan placed *after* acquisition with the real estate as collateral. The "antideficiency" laws apply to "purchase money" loans (loans taken on by a purchaser) when the property is acquired. Only then is it true that the lender has *no recourse* to the buyer.

In Georgia, however, purchases are "without recourse" only if the written agreement expressly lays it out as being "without recourse." If nothing is said about it at all, the transaction is presumed to be "with" recourse. This means that if the lender doesn't get enough on resale after foreclosure, the lender can sue for the difference. In other words, the seller has recourse to *all* of the buyer's assets until the loan is fully satisfied.

If you're holding someone's note and about to foreclose, see your lawyer. If you foreclose using a private power of sale, the speedy approach to getting your property back, you might be waiving your right to a deficiency judgment. If you want a deficiency judgment, you might have to sue to get it (by way of "judicial foreclosure"). Such deficiency judgments, once obtained, are good for many years.

If you're a highly leveraged borrower in a hostile legal environment (one with deficiency judgments), then perhaps you should think twice about a "nothing down" deal. If you're overpaying for the property, you may be the king of the cocktail party today, but the guest of honor at the crocodile convention tomorrow.

After some reflection on this bleak opening, I can almost hear you asking me: "Well, just what do you expect me to do? I wouldn't be reading your book if I had a lot of equity and could buy myself a little cash flow and a rocking chair on easy street. Give me an idea of how to get started."

Patience, please. At this point, what I want you to see is that leverage is a double-edged sword. Nothing down deals may make the headlines when they're put together. They make only the inside pages when they fall apart.

3

Two, Two, Two Deals in One

The solution? The solution is to take advantage of the tax laws in a creative way; to work smart. The solution is what the pros call a "tax-structured" or "soft dollar" deal.

Although most people haven't dealt with soft dollars, professional investors realize that there are two deals to work out in every transaction: the *economic* deal and the *tax-structured* deal. The economic deal is the first one buyers and sellers tend to think about. After negotiation, buyers and sellers tentatively decide on a purchase price and the terms: the down payment and the terms of any notes. Even when the terms are "all cash," and there's no financing, however, there's *still* an opportunity to do some tax-structuring by building in soft dollars.

Most of us, of course, don't pay all cash. Instead, we pay something down and agree to pay the balance over time. The down payment is usually 20 percent cash, and the balance is usually in the form of a promissory note. The note may be unsecured, but it's more likely to be collateralized by a mortgage (or deed of trust) if we're buying real estate, or a security agreement if we're buying equipment or other tangible personal property, or a pledge agreement if we're buying shares of stock or other intangible personal property.

Basically, however, we're usually dealing with some cash and a note. This is all we need to worry about. We'll ignore the various ways to secure or collateralize the note.

The promissory note will contain many important provisions. For our purposes we care only about the essentials: the interest rate, the monthly payment, and the due date.

Let's not be too academic about this. Suppose we agree to the purchase of our hypothetical duplex for $100,000. It all boils down to deciding, for example, to pay $100,000 with, say, $20,000 cash down and a promissory note for $80,000, with terms. Typical terms might be interest only at 12 percent per annum payable in monthly installments of $800 ($80,000 × .12 = $9,600 ÷ 12 = $800 per month), or more,[1] all due five years after the closing. If the loan amortized principal and interest over thirty years, the monthly payment would be $822.90.[2]

Now maybe the down payment isn't 20 percent of the purchase price. Maybe it's only 10 percent. In that case, there's less need for tax-structuring and less to work with to accomplish the desired result. And you only have a little iceberg equity in the property. If you've worked out a "nothing down" deal with a break-even cash flow, then quit while you're ahead.

The reason I'm writing this book, however, is that a solid "nothing down" deal is almost a contradiction in terms. When you have nothing in the deal, you have nothing to lose. Many sellers realize this and raise the price to account for the risk that they might wind up with the property again after foreclosure. Most sellers want their buyers to have a stake in the property, so that they will fight against foreclosure for fear of losing their equity. Most of us, even the best of negotiators, wind up paying some portion of the purchase price in a down payment.

What's surprising, however, is that most of us stop thinking at this point. *That's the mistake.* There's lots more to do. The second step, the soft dollar step, is really part of those initial negotiations. You need some instruction in the techniques and a little imagination, however, to build them into the negotiations.

The essential idea is to carry out, by proper documentation, your true intentions. The economic deal must be negotiated in a way that takes advantage of the tax laws (regardless of what they may be) and achieves a better bottom-line result. In doing so, there are two aspects of the economic deal that must remain intact: We must give our seller the agreed purchase price and we must pay the agreed amount of cash.

Notice I said "cash," not down payment. We're going to leave the economic deal behind to some extent and, to free your mind from confining terms like "down payment," I'm going to refer only to paying the agreed-upon *cash*. As you'll see, I wasn't kidding when I said that the way to write off your down payment is not to make one. While it may seem like alchemy at the moment, you'll soon see what I mean.

Restructuring how the cash is paid is the key to creating soft dollars. If we pay our cash as a down payment in the economic deal, we have paid it in a way that produces only iceberg equity. Since equity can't be expensed (that is, written off as expense), there's no cheese at the end of this tunnel. The idea is to pay the agreed-upon cash in a combination of ways that result in services we truly need, and for which we will pay as first- or second-year expenses. Legitimate expenses, of course. *They* can be written off.

To the extent we convert down payment dollars to cash paid for other things we need, we *reduce* our down payment. If we take our strategy to the ultimate, we'll convert an economic deal *with* a down payment to a soft dollar deal with *nothing* down. Remember, however, that our level of debt is the same as if we were making the normal down payment. We don't want a nothing down deal with loans so high that we'd just be buying a croc (excuse the pun).

The magnificent upshot is that a tax-structured deal increases our tax loss (there are more expenses), reduces our iceberg equity (there's less money down), and increases our return-on-equity yield—all at the same time (because there's less money working to make the same profit). All this, and with no adverse impact on cash flow.

Before I go any further, let me digress to explain why I think most of us stop thinking after we reach the economic deal. Without any solid proof, admittedly, I think it's because we usually think of tax-structuring only when we're sellers. That's when we lawyers usually hear from our clients. Usually the sale is large and our clients want any gain to be a long-term capital gain. Only 40 percent of a long-term capital gain is taxable, so we care about making sure we've met the requirements, the chief of which is the proper holding period of a capital asset (only six months, as of June 22, 1984). When we *buy*, however, we don't think about the tax aspects, because that's mistakenly believed to be the sole province and concern of the seller.

It's time to stop this myopia. The tax aspects of any transaction are *always* important to both the seller *and* the buyer. A better tax structure to the deal can often make no difference at all to the seller, and *all the difference* to the buyer. Marginal deals become good ones. Good ones become great ones.

You don't have to be a tax lawyer to understand all this. I'm not. Stay with me and I'll show you how to negotiate better deals by making use of a few simple tools. At this point, put yourself in the position of a buyer and open your mind to the realization that we have work to do. First we have to agree on an economic deal. Then we have to go on to see what we can do to improve it by using the soft dollar techniques.

NOTES

1. The phrase "or more" means that the borrower is allowed to pay more than $800 per month, and this translates into meaning that there is no prepayment penalty when the loan is refinanced before maturity. The opposite situation would be a "lock-in" clause, which locks the borrower into the repayment schedule without being allowed to repay the lender. One middle ground is a specific prepayment penalty for an early payoff. In some cases, the loan can be structured so that a certain percentage of principal, say 20 percent, can be prepaid each year without penalty. This results in a declining prepayment penalty over time.

2. Mortgage tables are readily available for different interest rates, periods of amortization, and loan amounts. You can obtain them in most bookstores. In order to use these tables, you simply correlate the rate, maturity, and amount. For example, I looked up the table for 12 percent, and then correlated the column for thirty years with the amount of $80,000. The intersection of the rows and columns indicates the monthly payment. See the example in the following table.

MONTHLY AMORTIZING PAYMENTS   12%

AMOUNT OF LOAN	NUMBER OF YEARS IN TERM					
	25	26	27	28	29	30
$ 50	.53	.53	.53	.52	.52	.52
100	1.06	1.05	1.05	1.04	1.04	1.03
200	2.11	2.10	2.09	2.08	2.07	2.06
300	3.16	3.15	3.13	3.11	3.10	3.09
400	4.22	4.19	4.17	4.15	4.13	4.12
500	5.27	5.24	5.21	5.19	5.17	5.15
600	6.32	6.29	6.25	6.22	6.20	6.18
700	7.38	7.33	7.30	7.26	7.23	7.21
800	8.43	8.38	8.34	8.30	8.26	8.23
900	9.48	9.43	9.38	9.33	9.30	9.26
1000	10.54	10.47	10.42	10.37	10.33	10.29
2000	21.07	20.94	20.83	20.74	20.65	20.58
3000	31.60	31.41	31.25	31.10	30.98	30.86
4000	42.13	41.88	41.66	41.47	41.30	41.15
5000	52.67	52.35	52.08	51.84	51.62	51.44
6000	63.20	62.82	62.49	62.20	61.95	61.72
7000	73.73	73.29	72.91	72.57	72.27	72.01
8000	84.26	83.76	83.32	82.93	82.59	82.29
9000	94.80	94.23	93.74	93.30	92.92	92.58
10000	105.33	104.70	104.15	103.67	103.24	102.87
11000	115.86	115.17	114.56	114.03	113.58	113.15
12000	126.39	125.64	124.98	124.40	123.89	123.44
13000	136.92	136.11	135.39	134.76	134.21	133.72
14000	147.46	146.58	145.81	145.13	144.54	144.01
15000	157.99	157.05	156.22	155.50	154.86	154.30
16000	168.52	167.52	166.64	165.86	165.18	164.58
17000	179.05	177.99	177.05	176.23	175.51	174.87
18000	189.59	188.46	187.47	186.60	185.83	185.16
19000	200.12	198.93	197.88	196.96	196.15	195.44
20000	210.65	209.40	208.29	207.33	206.48	205.73
21000	221.18	219.87	218.71	217.69	216.80	216.01
22000	231.71	230.33	229.12	228.06	227.12	226.30
23000	242.25	240.80	239.54	238.43	237.45	236.59
24000	252.78	251.27	249.95	248.79	247.77	246.87
25000	263.31	261.74	260.37	259.16	258.09	257.16
26000	273.84	272.21	270.78	269.52	268.42	267.44
27000	284.38	282.68	281.20	279.89	278.74	277.73
28000	294.91	293.15	291.61	290.26	289.07	288.02
29000	305.44	303.62	302.03	300.62	299.39	298.30
30000	315.97	314.09	312.44	310.99	309.71	308.59
31000	326.50	324.56	322.85	321.36	320.04	318.87
32000	337.04	335.03	333.27	331.72	330.36	329.16
33000	347.57	345.50	343.68	342.09	340.68	339.45
34000	358.10	355.97	354.10	352.45	351.01	349.73
35000	368.63	366.44	364.51	362.82	361.33	360.02
40000	421.29	418.79	416.58	414.65	412.95	411.45
45000	473.96	471.13	468.66	466.48	464.57	462.88
50000	526.62	523.48	520.73	518.31	516.18	514.31
55000	579.28	575.83	572.80	570.14	567.80	565.74
60000	631.94	628.18	624.87	621.97	619.42	617.17
65000	684.60	680.52	676.95	673.80	671.04	668.60
70000	737.26	732.87	729.02	725.63	722.66	720.03
75000	789.92	785.22	781.09	777.46	774.27	771.46
80000	842.58	837.57	833.16	829.30	825.89	

4

Tools of the Trade

Now that we've discussed equity and leverage, let's look directly at situations in which we're asked to give 20 percent or 30 percent of the purchase price as a down payment and see what we can do about it. Before I begin, let me remind you that a tax-structured deal is possible for real estate investments (see Chapters 14 and 15) and for buying a business (see Chapter 16), as well as for the home you want to buy to live in. In the next few chapters I'll explain some of the tools available to accomplish these different tasks. Then I'll work through several examples of transactions structured to take advantage of these ingredients.

A soft dollar deal requires a clear understanding of the two most obvious ingredients: depreciation and the investment tax credit. These are tax losses or credits that aren't dollars out of your pocket.

As you probably realize, there are several investments that are encouraged by Congress and that get special treatment in the tax laws. Real estate is one of these. The hallmark is depreciation of everything except the land (which theoretically never depreciates). Another favorite is tangible personal property, a fancy category that usually boils down to cars, computers, furnishings, and equipment. Such tangible personal property is not only depreciable but also entitled to a first-year writeoff called an Investment Tax Credit or "ITC."

I'm going to explain these classic devices, and a few more. We'll develop a cookbook of ideas that we can pull down and examine each time we analyze a deal. A few will apply to buying a home. All of them will apply to making an investment or buying a business.

The fun is in cooking up the deal.

5

Appreciating Depreciation

Depreciation is a paper transaction. There is no drain on cash flow, but nevertheless, for tax purposes, depreciation is an expense. Theoretically, depreciation is an allowance for the future investment required to replace the used-up, worn-out structure. In practice, a structure or piece of equipment is fully depreciated more than once. I'll explain this in Chapter 6. Before I do, let's examine depreciation. For convenience, I'll refer only to structures. We'll cover the depreciation of equipment later.

In a real estate context, you start out with the cost of the structure. This is sometimes based on the relative values assigned to the land and the structure by the local tax assessor (when it's to your advantage). Alternatively, the IRS will also honor an allocation between land and structure made by the buyer and seller in their written agreement, so long as it's the reasonable result of an "arm's length" negotiation (one in which buyer and seller have substantial and opposite interests).[1] I'd love to depreciate 100 percent of the purchase price, but that would be equivalent to assigning a value of zero to the land. If I were buying *only* the improvements and some other entity—a pension plan, for example—were buying the land, this would make sense. If I were buying land *and* building, however, this tactic would clearly be unreasonable, and after an audit would be overturned.

Let's work through a simple example to clarify the role of depreciation. I'm going to buy our familiar duplex as an investment for $100,000. The duplex is ten years old but in good condition. According to the local property tax rolls, the land and structure have values of $18,000 and $54,000 respectively. These may reflect an old transaction or a recent assessment.

39

The *relative* values (see Figure 5-1) are 25 percent and 75 percent, respectively.[2]

$$\frac{\text{Land}}{\text{percentage}} = \frac{\text{Land}}{\text{Total}} = \frac{\$18,000}{\$18,000 + \$54,000} = \frac{\$18,000}{\$72,000} = 25 \text{ percent}$$

$$\frac{\text{Structure}}{\text{percentage}} = \frac{\text{Structure}}{\text{Total}} = \frac{\$54,000}{\$72,000} = 75 \text{ percent}$$

Figure 5-1.   Hypothetical Land-Structure Percentages.

What this tells us is that we can depreciate $75,000 (75 percent of $100,000). This is the initial value assigned to the structure for depreciation purposes *when there is no other agreement.* The formula is:

Purchase price × percent allocated to structure = initial value of structure ($100,000 × 75 percent = $75,000).

For most investors, this is a reasonable approach, which the IRS doesn't debate—as long as the allocation to the structure is reasonably related to its value. Let's make an agreement with the seller to allocate the purchase price between the land and the structure in a way favorable to us. This involves nothing more than saying "I'll pay so much for the land and so much for the structure." This agreement appears in the contract in a straightforward sentence: "Buyer and Seller hereby agree to the following allocation of the purchase price to the land and structure respectively: $15,000 for the land; $85,000 for the structure."

Notice that I've changed the deal. I'm being aggressive, as a tax planner, and allocating 85 percent of the value to the structure. An appraisal by a qualified professional should be obtained to substantiate the allocation. Even without an appraisal, a deal that can be shown to be the result of good faith bargaining by persons with substantial and opposite interests should stand up. Let's see how the change affects the tax aspects in our first year of ownership.

There are two basic methods of calculating depreciation. The first is called straight-line. This formula allows for an equal amount of depreciation each year for the allowable term, which is eighteen years. Using the straightforward, straight-line approach, and assuming no salvage value, the $75,000 structure will completely depreciate (legally wear out) over the allowable term of eighteen years. In each year, then, the depreciation is $4,167. The formula is:

$$\frac{\text{Structure Value}}{\text{Term}} = \frac{\$75,000}{18 \text{ yrs}} = \$4,167 \text{ per year.}$$

By changing the allocation, I can increase my depreciation writeoff for each and every year by $555. The calculation is:

$$\frac{\text{Structure Value}}{\text{Term}} = \frac{\$85,000}{18 \text{ yrs}} = \$4,722 \text{ per year.}$$

This is an extra $555 ($4,722 − $4,167) or 13.3 percent in depreciation expense ($555 ÷ $4,167), and I obtained it simply by bargaining for it. I say it's this simple because this is one request that can make a difference to the buyer, but usually makes no difference to the seller.[3] The seller pays tax on that portion of the purchase price actually received that represents gain. It usually doesn't matter whether the seller is getting paid for the land or for the structure: The total amount received is all that the seller cares about. So this allocation, which can favor a buyer and make a marginal deal feasible or a sweet one sweeter still, is relatively easy to obtain. It may cost the seller nothing. The buyer must simply remember to ask for it and to be able to substantiate it.

One other tidbit. Although IRS regulations require an allocation[4] of basis (a technical tax term essentially meaning cost) in accordance with the relative values of the land and improvements respectively, the form for reporting depreciation (Form 4562; see Figure 5-2) does not require that you disclose the percentage that you used or your ability to substantiate it. You simply record the amount ("cost or other basis") being depreciated.

We've now discussed the first ingredient in our soft dollar cookbook: allocations. Sophisticated real estate investors love to

Figure 5-2.

Form **4562**	**Depreciation and Amortization**	OMB No. 1545-0172
Department of the Treasury Internal Revenue Service (O)	▶ See separate instructions. ▶ Attach this form to your return.	**1984** 67

Name(s) as shown on return		Identifying number

Business or activity to which this form relates

Part I Depreciation	For transportation equipment (e g. autos), amusement/recreation property, and computer/peripheral equipment placed in service after June 18, 1984, and used 50% or less in a trade or business, the section 179 deduction is not allowed and depreciation must be taken only on line 2(h).

Section A.—Election to expense recovery property (Section 179)

A. Class of property	B. Cost	C. Expense deduction

1 Total (not more than $5,000). (Partnerships or S corporations—see the Schedule K and Schedule K-1 Instructions of Form 1065 or 1120S) . . . .

Section B.—Depreciation of recovery property

A. Class of property	B. Date placed in service	C. Cost or other basis	D. Recovery period	E. Method of figuring depreciation	F. Deduction
2 Accelerated Cost Recovery System (ACRS) (see instructions): *For assets placed in service ONLY during taxable year beginning in 1984*					
(a) 3-year property					
(b) 5-year property					
(c) 10-year property					
(d) 15-year public utility property					
(e) 15-year real property—low-income housing					
(f) 15-year real property other than low-income housing					
(g) 18-year real property					
(h) Other recovery property				S/L S/L	

3 ACRS deduction for assets placed in service prior to 1984 (see instructions) . . . .

Section C.—Depreciation of nonrecovery property

4 Property subject to section 168(e)(2) election (see instructions) . . . .
5 Class Life Asset Depreciation Range (CLADR) System Depreciation (see instructions) . . . . .
6 Other depreciation (see instructions) . . . .

Section D.—Summary

7 Total (Add deductions on lines 1 through 6). Enter here and on the Depreciation line of your return (Partnerships and S corporations—DO NOT include any amounts entered on line 1.) . . . .

Part II Amortization

A. Description of property	B. Date acquired	C. Cost or other basis	D. Code section	E. Amortization period or percentage	F. Amortization for this year

Total. Enter here and on Other Deductions or Other Expenses line of your return . . . .

See Paperwork Reduction Act Notice on page 1 of the separate instructions.   ⬦ U.S.GPO 1984-0-423-236   E I #430814328   Form **4562** (1984)

make allocations because they increase depreciation writeoffs and because auditors tend to accept allocations that resulted from contract negotiations and are "in writing."

Ingredient 1:   Allocate.

NOTES

1. Although a local tax assessor might assign 60 percent of the value to the improvements and 40 percent to the land, an appraisal by a qualified professional might assign 80 percent of the value to the improvements. And an insurance agent might honestly believe that the replacement value of the structure is 88 percent of the purchase price. The following are a few court cases on this issue: *Meiers* v. *Comm.*, 43 TC Memo 454 (1982) (upheld 80 percent allocation of purchase price to buildings based on cost of replacement valuation); *Comm.* v. *Gazette Telegraph Co.*, 19 TC 692 (1952), *aff'd*, 209 F.2d 926 (10th Cir. 1954), 45 A.F.T.R. 266, *acq.* 1954-2 Cum. Bull. 4 (upheld allocation between stock and covenant not to compete because they were valued and documented separately; *but see Particelli* v. *Comm.*, 212 F.2d 498 (9th Cir. 1954) (rejecting allocations as "window dressing"), and *Meeker* v. *Comm.*, 41 TC Memo 1409 (1981) (denied 40 percent allocation based on arbitrary "rule of thumb").

2. Remember that these relative values can be substantiated with a tax assessor's valuation, by a do-it-yourself appraisal (not recommended), by a professional appraisal, or by an agreement reached in an arm's length transaction.

3. If the seller has been using accelerated depreciation, the allocation *will* make a difference. A higher allocation to the structure will increase the amount of depreciation recaptured as ordinary income, a subject covered in Chapter 6. Where sellers have been using straight-line depreciation, however, there is no recapture.

4. Reg.§1.167(a)-5.

6

Depreciation in Detail

Once we've made an allocation we turn to the method of depreciation. Because this important concept has a number of complex variations, we must digress to explore the various details. Even before there was a federal income tax, the business community was using the concept of depreciation. In the Internal Revenue Code, Sections 167 and 168 treat depreciation as if it were an operating expense by allowing an annual deduction for wear and tear. Because you can only deduct depreciation for property used in a trade or business or property held for the production of income, you can't depreciate your home. Also, you can't depreciate raw land, because it theoretically doesn't wear out. Goodwill is also disqualified, because it has no ascertainable useful life.

In 1981, Congress passed the Accelerated Cost Recovery System, known as ACRS, which simplified the calculations. Before ACRS, each taxpayer had to determine how long a piece of equipment or an improvement to realty would be useful. That involved the selection of the "useful life." A taxpayer was allowed to write off the net "cost or other basis" over the useful life. That meant figuring out what the salvage value would be at the end of the useful life, subtracting it from cost, and dividing the remainder by the number of years it would take to completely expense it.

The textbooks show the formula for this relationship simply as:

$$\frac{\text{cost} - \text{salvage value}}{\text{useful life}} = \text{yearly depreciation.}$$

Because the useful life was chosen by the taxpayer, and because there are several variations on the theme (the classic formula is called "straight-line" depreciation), Congress passed the ACRS system to remove the guesswork. For example, salvage value is now ignored and doesn't figure in at all. Even more important, the ACRS system establishes a number of categories of depreciable assets and fixes the useful life for each one.

Categories. Tax planning is often about fitting into or choosing categories.

Before going into the details of ACRS, let me briefly describe the three principal methods of calculating depreciation. They are straight-line, the declining-balance method, and the sum-of-the-years-digit method. Straight-line has been described already and is the simple, straightforward way to write off the cost—by an equal amount each year. The declining-balance method involves applying the same *rate* of depreciation to the unrecovered basis. Since the "basis" each year is equal to the initial cost less depreciation already taken, the rate is applied to a constantly decreasing number, and there is a greater writeoff in the earlier years than in the later ones. Because the rate of depreciation can reach 200 percent of the straight-line rate, the declining-balance method has been called "accelerated depreciation." Besides a rate equal to 200 percent of straight line, there have been times when a taxpayer could select 175 percent, 150 percent or 125 percent, depending on the kind of property involved and whether it was new or used. Since ACRS, accelerated depreciation is still available, but the number of variations available has been reduced.

The third approach, the sum-of-the-years-digits method, has always been harder for people to grasp. It can best be illustrated with an example. The Senate Finance Committee explained it this way in 1954:

A acquires new property in 1954 which costs $175, has an estimated useful life of 5 years and an estimated salvage value of $25. The depreciation schedule for the asset will be as follows:

Year	Fraction of cost less salvage ($175 − 25 = $150)	Depreciation deduction	Adjusted basis
1	5/15	$50	$125
2	4/15	40	85
3	3/15	30	55
4	2/15	20	35
5	1/15	10	25

Most people have never bothered with this method.

As you can see, depreciation is a cost-spreading device that is not related to value. These depreciation methods are accounting conventions that operate rather mechanically. The taxpayer gets a return of his or her capital as the asset is expensed over time. Because of the rules, a taxpayer cannot time these deductions for convenience. What freedom a taxpayer has is determined *in the beginning* by choosing a depreciation method, after which the matter is fixed. There are primarily two degrees of freedom. The first is cost (which involves the allocation issue), and the second is the method of depreciation. The primary lesson for tax planning is to allocate the purchase price to establish a higher depreciable cost for each asset (Ingredient Number One), and then to select from the different methods of depreciation available.

Congress has been having a good time with the depreciation rules in the last few years. While the basic concepts—useful life, cost, the methods of straight-line and accelerated depreciation, and the adjustment of basis—still apply to all kinds of property, there are different rules for different types of property. The ACRS system was adopted in 1981 as a major part of the Economic Recovery Tax Act.

The ACRS system is mandatory. Basically, it's a set of pigeonholes: The one used depends on the kind of property involved. Once you know the rules, you can play the game. ACRS does *not*, however, apply to "intangible" property, which is nonphysical. A good example of an intangible is a consulting contract that calls for performance over a certain period. One does not depreciate an intangible; one "amortizes" it. And the rule is simple: An intangible must be amortized over its life using the straight-line method.

There are certain pigeonholes for tangible, depreciable property that are important. When one of them is appropriate, it must be used, and it determines the useful lives, which are referred to as "recovery periods." Most personal property falls into one of two categories: three-year property or five-year property. The classic example of a three-year property is the automobile. Light-duty trucks, special tools, and equipment used in research and experimentation also fit here. Just about everything else is five-year property. As for real estate, almost everything falls into the eighteen-year real property class. (I'm ignoring categories like fifteen-year public utility property, property used predominantly outside the United States, and certain railroad property.)

Let's focus on personal property for a moment. In particular, let's imagine that we've just bought a personal computer to keep track of our income and expenses. You can readily see that this is tangible and not a car. So it fits into the five-year property class. Because it does, we must use the various tables Congress has specified in Section 168(b)(1) of the Internal Revenue Code. We could, alternatively, use straight-line over five, twelve, or twenty-five years. If we do, then the election applies to all personal property within the class that we place into service during the year. Regardless of when that is, Congress has accepted a "half-year" convention (conventions are arbitrary rules that make life simple), which treats all property as if it were placed into service at the midpoint of each year, regardless of the actual date. The depreciation tables take this into account. To even things out, there is a "half-year" deduction (another convention) allowed for the year following the end of the normal recovery period.

There is one little trap that should be mentioned here. If the property is sold before the recovery period is over, the seller is allowed no deduction in that particular year or any succeeding year.

We can see the effect of the depreciation tables (the tables themselves are in Appendix A) if we continue with our hypothetical example. Let's imagine that the computer costs $3,200 new. In figure 6-1, you can compare the results for different methods of depreciation. (The figure also shows depreciation schedules for the rules before ACRS so that you see how the new system functions by comparison). Our example assumes that the useful life of the computer, but for ACRS, would have been eight years. Note that the ACRS deductions are sometimes smaller than would have been allowed using methods of accelerated depreciation, but that the entire cost is written off more quickly.

Pre-ACRS Methods

	Straight-Line		Declining-Balance		Sum-of-Years-Digits	
Year	Annual	Cumulative	Annual	Cumulative	Annual	Cumulative
1	400	400	800	800	712	712
2	400	800	600	1,400	622	1,334
3	400	1,200	450	1,850	534	1,868
4	400	1,600	338	2,188	444	2,312
5	400	2,000	252	2,440	356	2,668
6	400	2,400	190	2,630	266	2,934
7	400	2,800	142	2,772	178	3,112
8	400	3,200	108	2,880[a]	88	3,200

	ACRS 1981–1984		ACRS Straight-Line	
	Annual	Cumulative	Annual	Cumulative
1	480	480	320	320
2	704	1,184	640	960
3	672	1,856	640	1,600[b]
4	672	2,528	640	2,240
5	672	3,200	640	2,880
6	0	3,200	320	3,200
7	0	3,200	0	3,200
8	0	3,200	0	3,200

Figure 6-1. Comparative Depreciation Results Using Three Depreciation Methods (Pre-ACRS) and ACRS (five-year property under ACRS; otherwise, an eight-year useful life with no salvage value).

a. Section 167(e)(1) would allow the taxpayer to switch to straight-line to get the full deduction.

b. Notice that half of the cost has been expensed by the end of the third year. The half-year convention is plainly visible in the Annual column.

There's one other goody to mention with respect to personal property: bonus depreciation. This gets a bit complicated, so stay with me. Section 179 of the Internal Revenue Code creates bonus depreciation to encourage taxpayers to invest in tangible personal property that is purchased for use in the taxpayer's trade or business (commonly known as Section 38 property). Section 38 property is property that would qualify for an investment tax credit (see Chapter 7). Section 38 is the Code section that specifies which property is entitled to the credit. To keep things simple, I'll define tangible personal property as the stuff that would normally qualify for an ITC.

If we purchase that computer, for example, we're in business. It's tangible personal property purchased for use in a trade or business. Purchase, however, means purchase. Excluded are acquisitions from related taxpayers, certain non-recognition transactions (like exchanges), gifts, and inheritances.

The advantage of bonus depreciation is an earlier writeoff because the basis is adjusted for it. It is, in essence, a second kind of depreciation deduction. The limits of the bonus are being increased. In 1982, the maximum was $5,000. In 1986, and thereafter, you can take up to $10,000 in bonus depreciation. The limits do not apply to each piece of property, but to all of the qualifying property placed into service each year.

Let's suppose that our computer was the only such tangible personal property that we bought and that the year is 1986. Because of bonus depreciation, we could elect to treat the entire $3,200 cost as a Section 179 deduction and write it all off in year one. Because the unadjusted basis would be zero, there is nothing to depreciate (the bonus depreciation deduction always comes first). If the machine had cost $13,200, we could elect to deduct $10,000 under Section 179 and then compute depreciation of our five-year property using an adjusted basis of $3,200 (see Figure 6-1). If we hold the computer for the full five years, our total deductions will be the same as if there were no bonus. The effect of bonus depreciation is to change the *timing* of the writeoff, accelerating it. While $10,000 is no big deal if the machine is a nuclear magnetic resonating scanner (costing $1.5 million), it's very powerful for smaller transactions.

Even so, bonus depreciation has a few thorns. To the extent that Section 179 is used to write off our computer, for example, we lose our investment tax credit. We'd get an ITC computed only against $3,200, not against $13,200. In addition, because it's another kind of *accelerated* depreciation deduction, it is subject to recapture (which I'll soon explain) in the year of disposition (sale or exchange). Also, if the property is sold on an installment sale basis, the amount of bonus depreciation is deemed received in the year of sale, regardless of how much cash is received.

So much for personal property. Let's go on to real estate. Although ACRS has replaced the applicability of Section 167, for the most part, the old rules are worth a passing mention. Real estate used to be divided into four categories, because the Code distinguished between new and used and between residential and nonresidential. A building was residential if 80 percent of its gross rental income was from dwelling units (excluding hotels and any other building in which more than half of the units were used on a transient basis).

Under the Code, nonresidential (i.e., commercial) rental property could be depreciated using the straight-line method or the 150 percent declining-balance method (a variation on the 200 percent declining-balance method we discussed in connection with personal property). Used commercial property could be depreciated using only the straight-line method.

By comparison, the Code has always been a bit more favorable to residential income property. New residential rental property could be depreciated using straight-line, the 200 percent declining-balance method, or the sum-of-the-years-digits method. Used residential property could be depreciated using straight-line or the 125 percent declining-balance method.

ACRS uses a less complicated approach. First, most real property placed into service after December 31, 1980, is "eighteen-year property." Under ACRS, real property is either depreciated over eighteen years using the straight-line method or written off using the 175 percent declining-balance method and switching to straight-line at the appropriate time. The exact deductions are simply read from tables published by the Treasury (see Tables 4 and 5 in Appendix A). With respect to accelerated depreciation, the tables handle everything, because ACRS no longer makes the new–used, residential–nonresidential distinctions.

However, the distinction is very important when it comes to the subject of "recapture." Recapture is a "gotcha." Under the old rules, the idea was that a taxpayer would have to pay for using accelerated depreciation when the property was sold. At that time, the difference between straight-line depreciation and accelerated depreciation was "recaptured." What was an expense in the early years became *ordinary income* when the property changed hands.

In order to encourage investment in residential income property, ACRS handles recapture in a way that is treacherous for the unwary. For residential income property, there is still recapture, and it is still the difference between straight-line and accelerated depreciation. This amount is recaptured as ordinary income. For nonresidential (commercial) property, however, the use of accelerated depreciation is very expensive at the back end of the deal because *all* of the depreciation taken (not just the difference between straight-line and accelerated) is recaptured as ordinary income.

The Code speaks thusly: For commercial property, use straight-line depreciation; for residential income property, it's okay to use accelerated depreciation if you like (many prefer straight-line), because the cost is not prohibitive.

Those are the major features, but real property and personal property are treated slightly differently, and you should be aware of the differences. First, there is no "class" determination. The elections are made on a property-by-property basis. Second, there is no half-year convention. When a property is acquired, it can be depreciated according to the number of months it is used that year. The same is true in the year of disposition (the year of sale or exchange). Recapture is the "gotcha" if a taxpayer wants to use accelerated depreciation.

Now that we've chugged through the rules, past and present, let's see how to handle depreciation. The first thing to do is to reread the first paragraph in this chapter in order to find out what we don't want to pay for. The answers are homes (this is hard to avoid), raw land, and goodwill.

There are some interesting battles, of course, as lawyers try to structure deals for rapid writeoffs. For example, in *KFOX, Inc.* v. *U.S.,*[1] the cost of a radio station's personal service contracts were separated from goodwill in order to amortize them. Goodwill, you may recall, cannot be written off. Goodwill is iceberg equity. The contracts were amortized over the term in the contracts plus the period of a single renewal option. The IRS fought it, but lost, partly because the IRS has sometimes taken renewal and reserve provisions into account when determining "useful life."[2]

And in *Computing and Software, Inc.* v. *Comm.,*[3] the buyer of a consumer credit information service allocated part of the purchase price to the credit information files and lived to tell the tale. They were held to have an economic life of six years and could therefore be separated from goodwill (which is theoretically indefinite).

One strategy, therefore, is to stay away from (that is, allocate the purchase price to anything but) land in a real estate deal or to goodwill in a business acquisition. Of course, unreasonable allocations or allocations that have no economic basis (which is another way of calling them unreasonable) may be overturned as a sham. Nevertheless, the strategy, though aggressive, has precedent.

Second, as between tangible personal property and real property, it is obvious that five-year property can be written off more quickly than eighteen-year property. While a buyer might want to allocate away from land, he or she might want to allocate in the direction of personal property. This is usually hard to do to any great extent, but it can be done with recitals in the agreement, a detailed inventory, an allocation, and a bill of sale. With substantiation in the form of an appraisal, your chances of success are good.

Third, don't forget to allocate to intangibles when they have a sound economic reason for being. Take advantage of the more rapid writeoff schedule than ACRS affords for real estate. You design the agreements, including the term. You're entitled to amortize an allocation to an intangible like a personal service agreement (for example, a consulting contract) over the agreement's useful life—which you specify.

Now that we've explored these nuances of depreciation, we can mention the really Alice in Wonderland aspect of it all. The same property can be depreciated *more than once*. The depreciation expense is a theoretical world in which we supposedly take a dollar of depreciation expense and tuck it away into an ever-growing reserve fund to be used when our building has collapsed from age. Since structures can last forty years and longer, an eighteen-year depreciation period is the government's answer to an investor's prayers. In fact, the period is really designed to attract capital to residential income housing and commercial buildings, with a further bias in favor of housing (because of the way recapture has been designed).

Depreciation is unrelated to the physical structure in yet another way. Each buyer starts fresh. The ten-year-old duplex in our hypothetical example has no mileage whatsoever on it, even if it was fully depreciated by its previous owner.

Now that we've covered depreciation, we can add several more ingredients to our cookbook:

Ingredient 2:   Allocate to tangible personal property (cars, three years; most other property, five years).

Ingredient 3:   Allocate to intangibles (that is, agreements that can be amortized over their stated or economic life).

Ingredient 4:   For residential income property, use straight-line depreciation over eighteen years (no recapture) or accelerated depreciation (the recapture on resale is the difference between accelerated and straight-line methods).

Ingredient 5:   For commercial property, use straight-line depreciation over eighteen years.

NOTES

1. 510 F. 2d 1365 (Ct. Cl. 1975).

2. *See Comm.* v. *Pittsburgh Athletic Co.,* 72 F.2d 883 (3d Cir. 1934).

3. 64 TC 2. (1975) (CCH Decision No. 33,197).

7

Roll the Credits

Tangible personal property deserves more attention. It is almost always a significant part of any real estate purchase or business acquisition and it is almost always overlooked. It offers an even more rapid depreciation schedule and the availability of an investment tax credit in the first year of ownership. (The form you use to claim an investment tax credit is Form 3468, reproduced here as Figure 7-1.)

Tangible personal property includes the furniture, fixtures, furnishings (carpets, drapes, and so forth) and all that equipment, from the rake and garden hose to the office manager's personal computer.[1] Professionally, all of this stuff is often referred to as FF&E, which stands for "furniture, fixtures, and equipment." Intangible property, on the other hand, is best understood as stationery. A stock certificate, for example, is personal property, as opposed to real estate, but intangible, as opposed to a truck.

Under the Economic Recovery Tax Act of 1981, Congress retained the investment tax credit and liberalized it. (Excess credits can be carried back for three years [use Form 1040X for amended returns] or forward for fifteen years.) Although the rules are not as simple as the following summary suggests, the ITC rules are essentially these:

- There is a 6 percent ITC for three-year property.
- There is a 10 percent ITC for five-year and ten-year property, and for fifteen-year public utility property.
- There is a limitation for the ITC when used property is acquired. For the years 1981 through 1984, the credit is limited to $125,000 (it used to be $100,000). The plan was that, for prop-

Figure 7-1.

Form **3468**	**Computation of Investment Credit**	OMB No. 1545-0155
Department of the Treasury Internal Revenue Service (O)	▶ Attach to your tax return. ▶ Schedule B (Business Energy Investment Credit) on back.	19**84** 24

Name(s) as shown on return	Identifying number

Part I   Elections (Check the box(es) below that apply to you (See Instruction D).)

A   I elect to increase my qualified investment to 100% for certain commuter highway vehicles under section 46(c)(6) . . . . ☐

B   I elect to increase my qualified investment by all qualified progress expenditures made this and all later tax years . . . . . ☐
   Enter total qualified progress expenditures included in column (4), Part II ▶ . . . .

C   I claim full credit on certain ships under section 46(g)(3) (See **Instruction B** for details.) . . . . ☐

Part II   Qualified Investment (See instructions for new rules on automobiles and certain property with any personal use)

1 Recovery Property			Line	(1) Class of Property	(2) Unadjusted Basis	(3) Applicable Percentage	(4) Qualified Investment (Column 2 x column 3)
Regular Percentage	New Property		(a)	3-year		60	
			(b)	Other		100	
	Used Property		(c)	3-year		60	
			(d)	Other		100	
Section 48(q) Election to Reduce Credit (instead of adjusting basis)	New Property		(e)	3-year		40	
			(f)	Other		80	
	Used Property		(g)	3-year		40	
			(h)	Other		80	

2 Nonrecovery property—Enter total qualified investment (See instructions for line 2)	2	
3 New commuter highway vehicle—Enter total qualified investment (See **Instruction D(1)**)	3	
4 Used commuter highway vehicle—Enter total qualified investment (See **Instruction D(1)**)	4	
5 **Total qualified investment in 10% property**—Add lines 1(a) through 1(h), 2, 3, and 4 (See instructions for special limits)	5	
6 Qualified rehabilitation expenditures—Enter total qualified investment for:		
a 30-year-old buildings	6a	
b 40-year-old buildings	6b	
c Certified historic structures (You must attach NPS certification—see instructions).	6c	

Part III   Tentative Regular Investment Credit

7 10% of line 5	7	
8 15% of line 6a	8	
9 20% of line 6b	9	
10 25% of line 6c	10	
11 Credit from cooperatives—Enter regular investment credit from cooperatives	11	
12 Regular investment credit—Add lines 7 through 11	12	
13 Business energy investment credit—From line 11 of Schedule B (see back of this form)	13	
14 Current year investment credit—Add lines 12 and 13	14	

Note: If you have a 1984 jobs credit (Form 5884), credit for alcohol used as fuel (Form 6478), or employee stock ownership plan (ESOP) credit (Form 8007), in addition to your 1984 investment credit, you must stop here and go to new **Form 3800**, General Business Credit, to claim your 1984 investment credit. If you have only the investment credit (which may include business energy investment credit) or an investment credit carryforward from 1983, you may continue with lines 15 through 22 to claim your credit.

15 Carryforward of unused regular or business energy investment credit from 1983	15	
16 Total—Add lines 14 and 15.	16	

Part IV   Tax Liability Limitations

17 **a** Individuals—From Form 1040, enter amount from line 46 . . . .
   b Estates and trusts—From line 26a, plus any section 644 tax on trusts .
   c Corporations—From Form 1120, Schedule J, enter tax from line 3 (or Form 1120-A, Part I, line 1).
   d Other filers—Enter tax before credits from return . . . .
	17	

18 **a** Individuals—From Form 1040, enter credits from line 47, plus any orphan drug, nonconventional
     source fuel, and research credits . . . .
   b Estates and trusts—From Form 1041, enter any credits from line 27d .
   c Corporations—From Form 1120, Schedule J, enter credits from lines 4(a) through 4(e) (Form
     1120-A filers, enter zero) . . . .
   d Other filers—See instructions for line 18d . . . .
	18	

19 Income tax liability as adjusted (subtract line 18 from line 17).	19	
20 **a** Enter smaller of line 19 or $25,000. (See instructions for line 20)	20a	
b If line 19 is more than $25,000—Enter 85% of the excess.	20b	
21 Investment credit limitation—Add lines 20a and 20b	21	
22 Total allowed credit—Enter the smaller of line 16 or line 21. This is your **General Business Credit** for 1984. Enter here and on Form 1040, line 48; Form 1120, Schedule J, line 4(f); Form 1120-A, Part I, line 2 ; or the proper line of other returns	22	

For Paperwork Reduction Act Notice, see separate instructions.   Form **3468** (1984) erty placed in service at any time after January 1, 1985, the limit would increase to $150,000 per year. In 1984, Congress postponed the increase to 1988. At this time, it's still $125,000.

• Recapture applies. Although the credit is taken in the first year of service, only 2 percent is earned for each full year of use. For example, if three-year property is kept for the full three years, there is no recapture. Similarly, if five-year property is kept for the full five years, there is no recapture. If five-year property is kept for only three and one-half years, there is a recapture equal to the full credit (10 percent) minus 2 percent times the three full years of use (i. e., 10 percent − (2 percent × 3) = 4 percent).

All of this stuff needs to be inventoried and valued before the closing and this affords another opportunity to make an allocation. In so doing, we'll shift dollars from an eighteen-year depreciable term to a five-year schedule. Although only a small percentage of the purchase price is going to be FF&E, every little bit helps.

In our $100,000 duplex, let's assume that 5 percent of the purchase price ($5,000) is allocated to the coin-operated washers and dryers and see what happens. We'll assume that it's 1986 and use 200 percent accelerated depreciation (see Table 3 in Appendix A). First, we lose some of our depreciation expense. Instead of an $85,000 allocation to our structure, we now have a structure value of only $80,000. Our annual depreciation (straight-line over eighteen years) will go from $4,722 ($85,000 ÷ 18) to $4,444 ($80,000 ÷ 18).

But there is now $5,000 in FF&E. In the first year, we'll lose $278 in structural depreciation expense, but gain $1,000 ($5,000 × .20) in FF&E depreciation and a $500 ITC. By a mere allocation, we picked up another $722 in net depreciation writeoffs and a $500 ITC to boot.

Why is this? First, FF&E is five-year property under the Internal Revenue Code. That means it can be depreciated over five years. My $1,000 figure is the result of depreciating $5,000 over one year using Table 3 in Appendix A. Second, the ITC is a first-year benefit of 10 percent of the purchase price. The ITC is, however, also subject to recapture if the FF&E is sold during the ensuing five years. If it is held longer, there's no recapture. The depreciation taken on tangible personal property is recaptured, however, whenever the stuff is sold.

Before I log the ITC ingredient, we should be a bit more specific about Ingredient 2 (allocations to personal property): When allocating to tangible personal property, remember to allocate a portion of the purchase price to furniture, fixtures, and equipment (FF&E). Inventory all of it. Depreciate FF&E over five years (three years for automobiles). Then use Ingredient 6 (the ITC).

Remember, however, that if you're involved in a partnership, the benefits first reach the partnership level intact, but do not pass to investors without being parceled out. For example, let's suppose that we're buying a fancy piece of equipment. There's a fancy device, now being marketed, called a Nuclear Magnetic Resonating Scanner ("NMRS"). It's used in medical research to give doctors a picture of differing tissue masses (they resonate differently) without surgery. The patient merely sits in a magnetic field. The "nuclear" in the title refers to the nucleus of an atom, not radiation or the use of uranium. A NMRS sells for $1.5 million. Since it's equipment and not a car, an NMRS falls into the five-year category for depreciation purposes and qualifies for an ITC.

If we formed a partnership, you and I, to buy one—fifty-fifty—the partnership would get an ITC of $150,000 (10 percent of $1.5 million). As individuals, we'd receive only our proportionate share, or $75,000 each.

> *Ingredient 6:*   Take an investment tax credit ("ITC") of 6 percent for three-year property and 10 percent for five-year property as a first year direct offset to taxes due (or as an increase in tax losses to be carried forward).

REVIEW

So far, we've listed six "tools of the trade." I want to review them here. The highlights are:

1. Make allocations between land, structure, and equipment. Allocate as much of the purchase price to depreciable property as is reasonable. Design the allocations to structure and tangible personal property so that they have a proper relationship. You have a right to make the allocations, but the proportions call for careful judgment and substantiation.

2. Consider using accelerated depreciation for residential income property (any apartment house or complex) to increase depreciation expense, but realize that the difference between accelerated and straight-line depreciation will be recaptured on sale as ordinary income. Many people (author included) prefer to use straight-line and avoid the potential audit and recapture issue altogether.

3. Use straight-line depreciation for commercial property (stores, offices). If you elect accelerated depreciation, you'll really pay for it later. All of the depreciation expense taken, not just the difference between accelerated and straight-line, is recaptured as ordinary income.

4. Depreciate the portions of the purchase price allocated to personal property such as automobiles, if any, and to furniture, furnishings, and equipment, using the more rapid schedules. Consider using accelerated depreciation (see Appendix A).

5. Elect bonus depreciation for tangible personal property (maximum $10,000) to accelerate first-year writeoffs, but remember the price: recapture as ordinary income (and a lower basis to depreciate).

6. Take an investment tax credit where available on tangible personal property: 6 percent for three-year property and 10 percent for five-year property.

NOTES

1. There have been quite a number of cases on the question of whether certain kinds of property are eligible for an ITC. Here's a partial list where the ITC was allowed (unless otherwise indicated):

Bank Equipment. Vault doors, walk-up and drive-up windows, and night deposit boxes. Not the booth. Rev. Rul. 65-79; *see* Reg. §1.48-1(a) and (e).

Billboards. National Advertising Co. v. *U.S.,* 507 F.2d 850 (Ct. Cl. 1974) (because removable).

Cars. If used for business at least 50 percent of the time, a car is eligible, but only for a proportionate share of the ITC. Cars used in connection with providing lodging are *not* eligible. IRC Section 48(a)(1)(B). But cars used in connection with transient lodging (hotels), are eligible. IRC Section 48(a)(3)(B).

Computer software. Texas Instruments, Inc. v. *U.S.,* 551 F.2d 599 (5th Cir. 1977).

Display racks and shelves. Found in retail investment property. Reg. §1.48-1(c).

Elevators and escalators. Includes electrical and mechanical equipment associated with the elevator or escalator. If located in apartment buildings, they are *not* eligible. In *Klingle Corp.* v. *Comm.,* 29 TC Memo 603 (1970), the taxpayer owned an apartment building with restaurant, ballroom, and newsstand. He converted all the elevators to electric and claimed an ITC. The court applied a "predominant use" test and looked at the number of square feet allocated to transient tenants, revenue generated, and a head count of people using the equipment, but held that the taxpayer's reliance on the head count alone was insufficient. *See* IRC Section 48(a)(1)(B).

Fences. Yes, if for theft prevention or livestock. Reg. §1.48-1(d)(4); *Dolph Spalding,* 66 TC 1017 (1976).

Fire extinguishers. Rev. Rul. 67-417.

Furniture. Yes, for offices, hotels, motels, industrial buildings, and retail buildings, but *not* for apartment buildings; *but see* Rev. Rul. 81-133, where a leasing company that leased furniture to apartment tenants, but didn't own the buildings, was allowed an ITC. The ITC would have been denied had the leasing company leased the furniture to the owner who in turn leased the furniture to the tenants.

Gardening equipment. Yes, whether it came with the building or was bought separately, but again, not for apartment (residential) buildings. Reg. §1.48(d)(2).

Generators. Rev. Rul 70-103.

Heating and air conditioning equipment. Yes, if used to heat or cool equipment, but no if used to heat or cool people. Reg. 1.48-1(e)(2) and Rev. Rul. 68-530. Space heaters. Rev. Rul. 70-103.

Law books. Kipperman v. *Comm.,* 36 TC Memo 146 (1977). The law library was used Section 38 property when the lawyer sold the books to a partnership.

Movable partitions. Rev. Rul. 75-178. *King Radio Corp.* v. *U.S.,* 486 F.2d 1091 (10th Cir. 1973).

Office equipment. Yes. Reg. 1.48-1(c), but must be used more than 50 percent of the time for business (ineligible if business is lodging).

Ornamental fixtures and pictures. As in a coat of arms, but not mere artwork. Senate Report Pub. L. 95-600, p. 117 (November 6, 1978).

Sewage systems in trailer parks. Johnston v. *U.S.,* 45 AFTR 2d 80-948.

Signs. Neon and other. Reg. 1.48-1(c), but not for apartment buildings. Movable signs and identifying symbols are OK. Pole signs embedded in concrete aren't. *Southland Corporation* v. *U.S.,* 42 AFTR 2d 78-6269.

Telephone poles. Yes if they're yours, but no if they're not or they're used for residential property. Reg. 1.48.1(d)(4).

Truck. Same as car. Rev. Rul. 78-439 denied ITC on a truck used by owner of apartment building (section 38 specifically excludes personal property used in providing lodging).

Vending machines. Yes, including plumbing and electrical connections associated with them. Coin-operated washers and dryers are eligible, even in apartment buildings. IRC section 48(a)(3)(C).

Wall-to-wall carpet. Yes, if it's tacked down, but no if it's glued (again, not eligible if used in providing lodging; section 38). Rev. Rul. 67-349.

8

Valuable Handshakes

There are several kinds of simple agreements that are often used in sophisticated deal-making to document the true intentions of the parties. Without going into great detail at this point on any of them, let me give a few examples.

A CONSULTING AGREEMENT

Your seller may know the neighborhood better than you do. You might be wise to pay $500 or $1,000 a month, in advance, for consulting services during the first six months or year of ownership. The agreement would obligate your seller to provide written *or* oral advice on an as-needed basis not to exceed an agreed-upon amount of time per month. The advice might cover, for example, the availability of other properties in the area, the names of reliable suppliers, and contacts with local realtors or industry trade associations.

In exchange for these services, you agree to pay the full amount of the contract price in advance (for example, $500 a month = $6,000 per year).

In our original negotiations, of course, such an agreement is a separate discussion. It must be bargained for in an honest way and it must have economic substance. But there are tradeoffs in all negotiations. The dollars required for this agreement could boost the cash needed to make the deal to a point where the whole thing could fall apart. One compromise, however, is to deduct the cash needed for the agreement from what was once thought of—in the initial conception by the seller—as the down payment. The idea is for the seller to get the same *total* amount of cash he or she wants while allowing the buyer to pay for other services the seller can offer. In this case, $6,000 is paid for the consulting agreement and, in the process, turned into an expense. The down payment is reduced in the tradeoff.

Over what period can this expense be written off? The answer is over the life of the agreement, something, fortunately, that is within your control during negotiations. The expense associated with an agreement (an intangible) must be amortized over its life. Since the life of our consulting agreement is only one year, we've just turned $6,000 of iceberg equity into $6,000 of first-year expenses. An example of a consulting agreement is given in Appendix B.

RENT-GUARANTEE AGREEMENT

Another contract often used is one in which the seller guarantees the level of rental income for the first year. Such a contract means that the seller will make up for any unanticipated shortfall in the rental schedule that was indicated to attract the buyer in the first place. After a year, the property is far more familiar to and controllable by a new owner. Since a rent-guarantee agreement is a valuable form of insurance and peace of mind, it has a value even if there is never a shortfall in rent. And it too can be paid for in advance with dollars that would otherwise have been wasted on the down payment. An example of a rent-guarantee agreement is given in Appendix C.

COVENANT-NOT-TO-COMPETE

A variation of a rent-guarantee agreement is the "non-competition" agreement, often referred to as a *covenant-not-to-compete.*

The idea behind this agreement is to ensure that your seller does not undermine the value of your purchase. You don't want your seller to engage in cutthroat competition with you by buying a building across the street and lowering the rents to the point where you might lose your property in foreclosure. Some unscrupulous sellers have been known to do this. They take a small down payment and a note secured by the property. Then they attract the tenants away with low rents next door and foreclose. They wind up with both your down payment and your property. To protect against this, a wise buyer will seek a covenant against such practices. Then, if the worst begins to take place, a buyer has the basis for a court injunction stopping the nefarious seller in his or her tracks.

Competition is, however, favored by the law and such covenants will be narrowly construed both as to time and place. A covenant-not-to-compete covering an entire state (except per-' haps for Rhode Island, because it is so small) would undoubtedly have trouble and might be held unenforceably overbroad. Similarly a covenant for even two years might face rough sledding because of its duration. In order to be enforceable, a covenant ought to be geographically limited to the county or city in which the property or business is located (or to a five- or ten-mile radius if the city or county is large), with a time limit of a year or less.

Fine. A short-term contract is just what we want anyway. Again, we'll pay for this covenant in cash at the close of escrow with what otherwise would be down payment dollars. The covenant will be for a year (or less) and we'll have another first-year expense. An example of a covenant-not-to-compete is given in Appendix D.

PROPERTY-MANAGEMENT AGREEMENT

Many sellers are honest, hard-working people who would agree to stay on and manage one of the properties in your portfolio for a short time. They have a vested interest in good management, especially if they've accepted a promissory note as part of the purchase price. If the property is well rented and well maintained, they have a better chance of getting paid. Independent property managers usually charge 4 to 6 percent of the gross rent received. There's nothing sacred about the formula, however, and nothing wrong with paying a fixed fee in advance plus a percentage. For our purposes, the fixed fee might be 2 percent of the projected rents paid in advance at the closing with the coming year's management to be done for 4 percent of the gross rent received.

A property-management agreement is very much like a consulting contract, except that the services are more hands-on. Once again, it must be independently valid. It must be part of the deal, not an afterthought. In the world of tradeoffs, however, it presents an opportunity to pay cash that can be amortized over the life of a short-term agreement instead of paying the same cash as a down payment.

An example of a property-management agreement is given in Appendix E.

I've now briefly outlined four different contracts for a buyer to negotiate with a seller. They're all valuable things for a buyer to want to have and pay for. To recap, they are:

- Consulting agreement;
- Rent-guarantee agreement;
- Covenant-not-to-compete;
- Property-management agreement.

The good news is that you can use any combination of these agreements in your deal, or all of them if you so choose. You're better off, I think, using a multiplicity of agreements and assigning a small amount of money to each one than trying to have any single agreement carry a large burden. A consulting contract for $100,000 may have no economic reality behind it (in comparison to marketplace rates). Without some reasonable economic basis, the IRS would be able to attack the agreement as a sham and disallow the expense.

The next topic is the purchase money promissory note. Because it's more complex, I'll discuss it in the next chapter.

To close this chapter, however, let's add:

Ingredient 7:   Negotiate agreements with short terms and cash paid in advance for services or rights (promises).

9

Wrapping Paper

In *How to Borrow Money Below Prime* (Simon and Schuster, 1985), I explained how to avoid being charged "points" by a lender. A "point" is a fee charged by the lender for making the loan and is equal to 1 percent of the amount loaned. A point is equivalent to interest paid. It's paid just once, at the beginning of the loan, and may be amortized over the life of the loan (the time the loan is outstanding).

In this chapter, I'm going to explain how to do the opposite: how and why to *create* points. After we discuss the basics of a purchase money note, I'll show you how to structure points *into* your deal. These are points that your seller will charge and you, as buyer, will pay. I know this sounds like I'm switching sides and joining the lenders. Good debaters, often to be perverse, frequently do that. In this case, as you'll see, I'm doing it to structure more soft dollars. And I'll be using the same cash we otherwise would have paid as a down payment.

A purchase money note is simply a part of the purchase price that the buyer pays to the seller. While it looks as if the seller is loaning the buyer money and taking a mortgage or trust deed as collateral, most people (and courts) view it differently. While a purchase money note may involve an interest rate, points, and other jargon from the world of lending, what's really going on is that the seller is giving the buyer credit to make payments over time. The price charged for this extension of credit is usually interest, including points. Since this is a method of paying the purchase price over time, the terms are open to negotiation without limitation. In California, this is called the time-price doctrine. Since there is no loan involved, the usury laws do not apply. This may not be the case in your state, however, as the usury laws do vary, and you'd be wise to research this area.

Working with the structure of seller financing is also called creative financing. If you think about it for a moment, you'll realize that, while the money is owed to the seller, the creativity is built in to aid the buyer.

Frequently, such seller financing involves a mortgage or trust deed that is junior or subordinate in priority to an existing first-position loan owed to a bank or savings and loan. In the jargon of real estate, if a seller is in second place, he or she has "taken back a second." If there are two mortgages or notes for which the property is the security, a seller might be "taking back a third." Generally speaking, a note given by a seller is called "paper," and seller financing involves "taking back paper."

The true measure, of course, of whether a third, fourth, or fifth is economically safe depends on the ratio of the total debt to the fair market value of the property, a figure usually established by a professional appraiser. This is the loan-to-value ratio. If a seller takes back paper such that the total debt, including seller financing, is 75 to 80 percent of the fair market value, there should be a sufficient margin of safety, regardless of whether the paper is junior to a number of other notes. The safety is theoretical, of course. The thinking is that the 20 to 25 percent differential represents the new owner's equity that could be lost by the buyer in foreclosure. This is the buyer's incentive to keep all of the notes currently paid.

While I want you to see the economic reality of a seller's position regardless of the priority involved, it must be said that first position is better than second, second better than third, and so on. Remember that a note ahead of yours might become all due and payable before yours. If the new owner can't pay it, someone superior to the seller will begin a foreclosure and threaten to wipe out the paper the seller took back. In these relatively rare situations, the seller must pay off the senior noteholder to preserve his or her own position.

The primary point, however, is that sellers are free to negotiate the terms of the paper they take back. With this freedom, there is room for creativity. After finishing this chapter, you'll see why seller financing has also been called "creative financing."

Initially, a seller might be willing to take a second or a third, specifying the interest rate, payment frequency and amount, and due date. Because they're not lenders, sellers may need to be reminded that the credit they extend is very much like a loan. Instead of paying some portion of the purchase price simply as cash down, we'll offer to pay some portion of that cash as points. Points are considered to be prepaid interest, which must be amortized over the life of the note (but see Chapter 12 for a better result when buying your personal residence). If the note is all due, say, in five years, the points can be amortized over that period. This is true even if the note is set up to amortize over a thirty-year period, a strategy designed to keep the monthly payments low enough to be affordable.

Since our goal is to trade down payment dollars for soft dollars to any extent we can, let's reconsider our note. Points are a percentage of the initial unpaid principal. According to the marketplace, points can vary from as few as two, for first-position financing, to as many as ten or twenty, for second-, third-, or higher position financing.

It's really not the points we care about; it's the amount of money involved. In order to stay within the realm of the marketplace, however, we want to avoid an unusually large number of points. If the number of points is to be relatively small, we can generate a larger amount of soft dollars only by increasing the size of the note. Since the total amount to be paid to the seller isn't going to change, we need to remember that what is owed the seller is not only our note, but also the note or notes that the seller owes to others.

The size of the note is increased by using what's called (hold your breath) an all-inclusive purchase money promissory note, or "all-inclusive" for short. All-inclusives are sometimes called "wraparounds." Same animal.

What is an all-inclusive? Simply put, it's a note that is larger than and *includes* (hence the name) all of the notes owed by the seller to others. It "wraps around" these other notes, which is why it's often called a "wraparound," or "wrap" for short. Note that these other notes are owed by the seller, not the buyer. Buyers do not assume these underlying notes, but take the property subject to them. The seller remains liable and may have a better credit relationship with the other noteholders.

These are solid reasons for using an all-inclusive format.

The *equity* in the all-inclusive note is the same, however, as if the seller simply took back a junior note. This can be seen readily by working through a simple example. We want to buy a duplex worth $100,000 with a first-position note of $50,000 owed to a bank and a second-position note of $15,000 owed to a private party. These two notes total $65,000 and would be described collectively as the "underlying debt." The loan-to-value ratio is 65 percent ($65,000 in loans; $100,000 in value). Most institutional lenders will not loan more than 75 percent of the value, because they want the owner to have a substantial stake in the property. Our seller is, therefore, almost "loaned up" as far as institutions are concerned. Because we need more financing, the seller will have to make it available. We're still in the world of "seller financing."

Let's say, now, that the first carries an interest rate of 10 percent and the second an interest rate of 12 percent. We'd like to buy this duplex and we have a good monthly income, but not much in the way of savings. The sellers start out by asking for "all cash to the loans," with the buyer to assume any existing loans. This means that they want to take their $35,000 equity in cash and to be relieved of their outstanding debts. The difference between the asking price and their debt is their iceberg equity.

Our hypothetical sellers are, however, flexible. We offer $5,000 down and a third-position note of $30,000 at 13 percent, with the seller to remain responsible for the existing loans. We'll take the property subject to those loans and be secondarily liable.

We'll even *suggest* the all-inclusive format. After thinking about it (and seeing their lawyer), our sellers counter with $5,000 down and a third-position *all-inclusive* note of $95,000 at 13 percent. Apparently, our sellers don't need all of their equity in cash, and the $5,000 cash down is acceptable.

Why is the all-inclusive format even more desirable than the third-position note we offered? Before we go through the calculations, notice that our sellers have finally gotten their iceberg equity working for them. They're finally going to earn something on their equity. The question is how much?

We offered an interest-only third of $30,000 at 13 percent. For the year, that's $3,900 in interest. That's a 13 percent yield to our sellers because they'll be earning $3,900 on a $30,000 loan.

With the all-inclusive format, the income and yield are higher. The loan is for $95,000 at 13 percent, which generates annual interest income of $12,350 ($95,000 × 13 percent), out of which our sellers will have to pay annual interest expenses (assuming, for simplicity, interest-only loans) on the first and the second. The first will cost $5,000 ($50,000 × 10 percent) and the second will cost $1,800 ($15,000 × 12 percent), a total of $6,800. Their net income is $5,550 ($12,350 in interest income less $6,800 in interest expense). This net interest income is $1,650 *higher* for the same $30,000 loaned, solely because our sellers are earning a 3 percent spread on $50,000 (we're paying them 13 percent and they're paying 10 percent) and a 1 percent spread on $15,000 (we're paying them 13 percent and they're paying 12 percent) during the year. While the sellers did lend their "credit" by remaining liable on the underlying notes, they still only loaned $30,000 of the purchase price. Thus, their yield is equal to the $5,550 net income divided by the $30,000 receivable (the equity is now an asset), a yield of 18 percent. This is certainly better (38 percent better) than the yield of 13 percent which was offered in the original approach to lending the same $30,000, and all because we simply restructured the paper.

At this point we see the advantage, *to the seller,* of the all-inclusive note format. The all-inclusive note is still a third-position note, however, with the other two underlying notes having priority. (Priority is usually determined from the dates the mortgages or deeds of trust securing the notes were made "of record" [recorded] against the property.) The equity in the all-inclusive ($95,000 − $65,000) is the same as the original $30,000 principal of a third-position note. This is how much we would have to repay in order to obtain a cancellation of the note and a reconveyance of the all-inclusive deed of trust, leaving us with just the first and second.

We are, however, going to pay still more because of the extra credit we seek from the sellers. The sellers are going to remain primarily liable on the underlying notes, and that's worth money. We're back to points. Most institutional lenders charge points when making a loan. A loan in third position is difficult for a bank or savings and loan to make. While it may be economically sound, it looks risky. The loan might have to come from a "secondary" lender, a mortgage company, thrift and loan, or private investor. They charge even more. The interest rate might be higher and there could be anywhere from zero to twenty points charged just to make the loan. If the seller is carrying a second, or any financing more junior in priority than that, points are not difficult to justify.

As things stand in our hypothetical example, our sellers have countered with $5,000 down and a $95,000 all-inclusive note format, which we can show is more expensive for us as buyers. We're still paying $5,000 as the down payment. Our sellers haven't mentioned charging points, because they don't think of themselves as selling money; they're just trying to make a deal. A charge in the form of points for the extension of credit is, however, justifiable.

While I think the following example is somewhat extreme, it'll illustrate my point. Instead of paying $100,000 for the property, let's offer $95,000. The deal will be *nothing down* and an all-inclusive note for $95,000.

Now for the terms of the note. The rate will be 13 percent as before, but we'll now specify the term as being two years and we'll propose that our seller charge 5.25 percent in points on the $95,000 all-inclusive. These points will result in a writeoff. The $5,000 in points will be amortized as an additional interest expense over the life of the loan (again, the rule is different for your personal residence; see Chapter 12). The $30,000 loan will have a life of two years and the points will result in a $2,500 expense in each of them. In each year, however, the expense is a paper writeoff, not dollars out of pocket. Those dollars were paid at the closing.

Why 5.25 percent? Because the $5,000 to be paid in points is, when divided by $95,000, equal to 5.26315 percent. Rounded, that's 5.25 percent. Now 5.25 percent times $95,000 only equals $4,987.50, and another $12.50 must be paid to exactly match the economic deal. This can be handled in a number of ways, perhaps the simplest of which is for the seller to charge $12.50 for preparing the promissory note.

The deal is now this: Nothing down with a $95,000 all-inclusive third-position note (wrapping a $50,000 first with interest at 10 percent and a $15,000 second with interest at 12 percent) bearing interest at 13 percent, plus 5.25 points paid at closing, plus $12.50 in advance as a document preparation fee. We paid $5,000, but instead of a deal with $5,000 paid down, we changed it into a "nothing down" deal. We paid the same cash ($5,000) but we paid it in a sophisticated way that allowed us to convert iceberg equity into soft dollars. Notice that our seller now has something better than the $40,000 iceberg equity—$5,000 in cash and a $35,000 equity in the all-inclusive ($95,000 due to the seller minus $65,000 owed) earning 13 percent.[1]

As we go further with all-inclusive notes in later examples, we'll see that seller financing in the form of an all-inclusive note is one of the most flexible and powerful devices at our command.[2] We can design the interest rate, the point structure, the term, and a prepayment privilege to recharacterize hard dollars—those nondeductible, iceberg equity dollars—into soft, deductible dollars. Almost at will.

We're now able to add yet another weapon to our arsenal:

Ingredient 8:   Use seller financing using all-inclusive notes involving points amortized over the life of the note.

NOTES

1. Because of the 3 percent spread on the $50,000 first and the 1 percent spread on the $15,000 second, the yield, or effective interest rate, is 18 percent.

2. After October 15, 1985, sales involving all-inclusives may involve a renegotiation of the interest rates stated in the underlying notes. This is because Congress, in the Garn-St. Germain Act, has made due-on-sale clauses enforceable. Since

many borrowers had relied on court decisions holding that the due-on-scale clause was not enforceable unless the lender could show an impairment of security, Congress allowed loans written during a "window period" to be assumed, even though they contained due-on-sale clauses. The window period stretched, generally, from 1978 to 1982. Loans written during those years could be assumed until October 15, 1985, when the window closed. The general rule now is that all loans are enforceable in accordance with their terms, including due-on-sale clauses. Due-on-encumbrance clauses, by which lenders can call a loan merely because the owner obtains additional financing, are still controversial.

10

Techniques of Interest

As you are no doubt aware, all of the interest that you pay on your home loan is deductible from your income. This has always been one of the top selling points of having your own home. Realtors rightly and often point out that rental payments on an apartment, or even the same home, can't be written off.

In addition to the deductibility of the interest paid on a home mortgage, virtually all other interest paid and accrued on real estate loans is deductible. The only categories of paid and accrued interest that aren't deductible are certain amounts of "investment interest"[1] and "construction period interest," neither of which play a significant role in the design of soft dollars.

In determining the amount of interest that can be deducted, the interest must be accrued and paid. Because of a change in the law in 1984, interest cannot be deducted unless it is both accrued and paid, regardless of whether a taxpayer reports income using the cash method or the accrual method.

Before exploring how to use interest to create soft dollars, it is crucial to understand what is meant by the terms "paid" and "accrued" as they relate to the deductibility of interest. These concepts can be understood more easily by reference to home mortgages. Afterward, we'll go on to investments.

Let's imagine that we have borrowed $100,000 to buy our home. We're being charged 12 percent on the loan. We are to repay the loan by paying interest only monthly, and then, at the end of five years, the entire principal.[2]

The notion of interest "paid" is understood by everyone who writes a check to make the monthly payment. In the case of our hypothetical loan, $1,000 in interest will be due each month, because a year's worth of interest is $12,000 ($100,000 times 12 percent equals $12,000) and one-twelfth of that is $1,000 per month. We'll be paying $1,000 per month until the due date (also called the maturity) of the loan. Each payment constitutes interest "paid."

Of course, not all loans require interest-only payments, as in the example above. Most loans made by banks and savings and loan associations are amortizing loans.[3] This means that along with monthly payments for interest, there are also payments for principal. A loan that fully amortizes will require payments that reduce the original principal to zero at maturity. Our hypothetical $100,000 home loan would be fully amortized in thirty years if all payments were equal for thirty years and the last payment covered the last bit of principal still owed. We'd have a party and burn the mortgage.

The monthly payments on the thirty-year amortizing loan would be roughly $1,029, a figure that is slightly greater than the $1,000 interest-only payment. At the end of the term of the interest-only loan, however, all of the original principal would still be due. This lump sum due is called a "balloon payment." There is no balloon payment on fully amortizing loans.

As has been said, the payment on the amortizing loan is roughly $29 more than the interest-only payment. This portion of the payment is a payment toward principal. As such, it is not deductible, because it is not interest paid. Only the interest portion of any note is deductible. Since an amortizing loan reduces the principal balance each time a payment is made, each successive payment is composed of less interest and more principal than the previous payment. This is an important point. In the early years, over 95 percent of each payment will go toward paying interest. After ten years or so, a more noticeable amount goes to repay principal. At the very end of the loan, most of the payment will not be deductible because most of it will go toward repaying principal.

From this example, we can see a number of principles that will help us appreciate how interest is paid on loans.

1. With an interest-only loan, there is no reduction in the principal balance as a result of the monthly payment.

2. With an interest-only loan, all payments will be interest paid.

3. With an amortizing loan, a portion of each payment is interest and a portion is principal.

4. With an amortizing loan, the portion of each payment that is principal is increased with each succeeding payment. Similarly, the portion of each payment that is interest is decreased. That means that the interest deductions available are *decreasing* each month.

Now let's consider what constitutes interest *accrued* on a loan. In calculating the amount of interest to be paid on our $100,000 interest-only loan, we had to determine how much was owed at the end of each month. For example, we computed that 12 percent of $100,000 was $12,000 and that one month's interest would be $1,000. At the end of the month, $1,000 in interest is due and payable. Whether or not it is paid, this is the amount of interest that has accrued. If all of the interest was paid every twelve months, instead of monthly, there would still be $1,000 in accrued interest at the end of each month.

Now let's say that our note is dated July 1, 1985, and that payment is due annually. On December 31, 1985, six months' interest has accrued for a total amount of $6,000. However, no payment is due, because the interest is to be paid at the end of the twelfth month. The annual payment of $12,000 isn't due until July 1, 1986. As a result, $6,000 accrued during the last six months of 1985 and $6,000 accrued during the first six months of 1986. Because interest wasn't paid in 1985, there is no deduction allowed because it wasn't paid then. When the $12,000 is paid in 1986, a $12,000 deduction can be taken, because $12,000 had accrued.

In order to maximize our interest deductions in 1985, then, we might consider paying interest on December thirty-first. If this were done, we could take the six months of accrued interest as a deduction in 1985 because it would have been both accrued and paid in 1985. For us to get the deduction, the interest must have accrued (in accordance with the note terms) *and* been paid during the year.

While it is typical for interest to be paid *after* it has accrued (that is, in arrears), there is nothing that requires this. For example, a note that requires an annual installment of interest to be paid at the end of the year easily could be rewritten to provide that the payment be made at the beginning of the year.[4] A note of this type calls for the prepayment of interest. Under the terms of such a note, interest is paid before it accrues. In our example, if we had paid $12,000 on the day we signed the note, none of the interest would have accrued. We cannot deduct this interest, even though we paid it, until it accrues. Because interest accrues based on the terms we build into our note, the terms become a matter of art, not routine. (There are two examples in the notes to this chapter.)

To finish our example, let us ask when the interest paid in advance will be deductible. The answer is that the deductions will exactly match the situation in which interest is paid in arrears. Since $1,000 accrues each month, $6,000 will accrue from July 1, 1985, to December 31, 1985, and another $6,000 will accrue from January 1, 1986, to July 1, 1986. We have the same result from the rate-of-accrual standpoint.

With this much under our belt, we can begin to see how prepaid interest can be a valuable ingredient in our cookbook. To appreciate the use of prepaid interest, however, we need to understand the development of the law as it relates to this issue.

Prepaid interest has been used by sophisticated tax planners for many years. Recognizing this, Congress has attempted to deal with the issue of interest deductions on a number of occasions. This tinkering has led to quite a few misconceptions about prepaid interest. It's time to set the record straight.

At one time, wealthy individuals could pay as much as *five* years' interest in advance and deduct all of it in the year paid. This was a bonanza for many highly compensated people. Suppose that interest was due on a $1 million note bearing 10 percent interest. Instead of paying the $100,000 in interest due, the wealthy few could afford to pay almost $600,000, the $100,000 due and almost $500,000 in advance. They made such payments around December thirty-first of each year and chopped their other taxable income to next to nothing (if not nothing).

In the early 1970s, the ability to deduct prepaid interest in this fashion was limited to no more than two years. However, this was still a tax planner's dream. Everyone rushed to close their escrow on December thirty-first of each year in order to generate deductions by prepaying two years' interest.

In 1976, Congress finally passed a law to curtail this abuse. Congress said that you could only deduct prepaid interest to the extent that it was accrued. Now you know why we've gone through the definitions so carefully.

There's one other major distinction to make. Taxpayers can calculate their income in one of two ways, using either the cash or the accrual method. Individuals must pay tax based on the cash method. Many businesses, however, report their income using the accrual method. This means that they count their receivables as income (before they get the cash) and their payables as expenses (before they pay the cash).

The accrual method became important during the late 1970s and early 1980s. Many real estate limited partnerships were formed to buy property using notes where the interest was not due to be paid until many years after it accrued. Even though the interest was not being paid, it was accruing. As a result, these partnerships would take deductions for which no cash had been expended, and these deductions were passed on to the individual investors. Because of special provisions in the law, they could take advantage of the benefit of accruing deductions at the partnership level when they couldn't have done the same thing as individuals.[5]

Congress recognized that many taxpayers were joining accrual partnerships to maximize interest deductions without actually spending any money. Thus, in 1984, Congress passed the Deficit Reduction Act and prohibited taxpayers from deducting interest that had accrued unless it was also paid. This was a special rule for interest deductions only. Accrual method taxpayers can still deduct many kinds of expenses that are accrued but not paid in the year they're deducted from income.

Out of this history we have today's basic rule: *Interest can only be deducted when the interest has been both accrued and paid.*

For every rule, there are exceptions. In this case, there are two exceptions worth mentioning. First, interest paid on loans while property is under construction cannot be deducted. This interest, known as "construction period interest," must be amortized over ten years. Only one-tenth of all such interest can be deducted each year, even though paid in the first year. Since we can't make much use of this, we won't consider it further.

The second exception involves "points," those little charges for making the loan. Points are paid at the time the loan is made. One point is one percent of the loan amount. Points can vary anywhere from one to fifteen or twenty. Since they're usually paid from the loan proceeds, the borrower gets less than the amount borrowed.

To review briefly the mechanics of points, let's continue with our familiar $100,000 loan. The lender might charge two points on the loan in addition to the 12 percent per annum rate of interest. That means a charge of 2 percent of the loan amount, or $2,000. Instead of being loaned $100,000, only $98,000 is disbursed. Even though these points are a cost of the money being borrowed, the lender doesn't call it interest and the IRS says that, generally speaking, loan points must be amortized over the life of the loan. This means that if the loan is a thirty-year loan, only one-thirtieth of the loan points can be deducted each year. Similarly, if the loan is for five years, only one-fifth is deductible each year.

Does the purpose of the loan make a difference? Yes. Here's the good news of Chapter 12 in advance. The exception to the exception is that loan points paid for a loan to buy or improve a personal residence are fully deductible when paid. The points are written off immediately instead of being amortized. Instead of being forced to write off one-thirtieth of $2,000, or $66.66 each year, the full $2,000 can be deducted.

Now that we've explored the basic rules, let's see how to use prepaid interest to create soft dollars. As we go into greater detail, this becomes somewhat complex. Read carefully.

The first opportunity for structuring soft dollars is a simple case of prepaid interest. If we reduce our down payment by an amount equal to prepaid interest, we have the ability to deduct, over some period, money that would have been part of the cost of the building. As we already know, depreciation is one of our most powerful ingredients, but the rules allow for a deduction of only about 6 percent of the cost of the structure per year. With prepaid interest, we can do much better.

Let's work through a different example to see how to structure prepaid interest into a deal. Let's consider a property for investment with a price tag of $1,250,000, for which the seller wants a $250,000 down payment together with a five-year note for $1 million. For simplicity at this point, assume that the $1 million note bears no interest.

Now for the negotiation. Instead of paying no interest, we propose to change the terms of the note so that it bears 4 percent interest for five years, with interest-only payments. This amounts to interest-only payments of $40,000 per year ($1 million times 4 percent per annum) and $200,000 during the five-year term. We aren't proposing to pay $200,000 more, however. We're proposing to pay $200,000 in prepaid interest and reduce the down payment to only $50,000. The price would be reduced by $200,000, to $1,050,000, as a result of the decrease in the down payment, but the cash paid at the closing would remain the same, $250,000, and the note given at the closing would remain the same, $1 million. Even though the note would call for 4 percent interest, there would be no payments to make because of the prepayment. Economically, then, our proposal is identical to the seller's.

Although there is no difference in the cash requirements or the consequences of the note, there is an enormous benefit to the buyer. In the original proposal, most of the $200,000 that would have been paid as part of the down payment would have been depreciable. Even assuming that all of it is depreciable, each dollar of down payment buys only approximately six cents in deductions (approximately $12,000) for the next eighteen years. When the same $200,000 is recast as interest, it is deducted as it accrues. Each year during the life of the loan, interest at 4 percent will accrue. Although no payments are due—they were prepaid—we'll have $40,000 in interest deductions in each of the next five years. The full $200,000 will be deducted over five years instead of over eighteen.

Our simplistic example demonstrates that we can deduct a portion of the down payment from the price and calculate the amount of interest payable over the life of the loan. If the term of the loan is shorter, more money can be deducted in each year. If the term had been four years, instead of five, the annual deduction would have increased to $50,000.

To calculate these deductions, a simple two-step process can be used. First, divide the total amount of interest by the number of years of the loan. This gives us the annual amount of interest payable. Then divide the annual amount by the loan amount to determine the rate:

1. Total prepaid interest ÷ loan term = annual interest;
2. Annual interest ÷ loan amount = interest rate.

Let's apply the formulas to determine the interest rate to be charged when the note term is reduced from five years to four. First, we divide $200,000 (the total prepaid interest) by four (the term) and find annual interest of $50,000. Now we divide $50,000 by the $1 million note and find that the interest rate must be 5 percent. If we wanted to deduct $200,000 over four years, we'd have to prepay $200,000 and write a four-year $1 million note that calls for 5 percent interest per annum. Similarly, if the loan were only for two years, the formulas tell us to use an interest rate of 10 percent per annum.

Our zero-interest loan is, generally speaking, unrealistic. Even when the seller initially wanted a certain amount of interest, however, we can still easily design the note to allow for prepaid interest, decreasing our down payment accordingly. We make exactly the same calculations as we did before and add the interest rate to the rate that would have been charged otherwise.

Let's suppose that our five-year note initially called for 9 percent (the initial rate), interest only payable monthly (which results in payments of $7,500 per month). We want to create $200,000 in soft dollars by using prepaid interest. When we made this calculation assuming a zero-rate note, we found that the rate that should be built into the note was 4 percent. The rate on our note would be the initial rate demanded, 9 percent, plus the rate associated with our prepaid interest calculations. As a formula, this is just: Note rate = initial rate + prepaid interest rate. When we apply this to our example, we find that the note should be written for 13 percent.

Now let's compare the initially proposed terms with our tax-structured deal:

Initial Terms

Price: $1,250,000

Down: $250,000

Five-year note: $1,000,000 bearing interest at 9 percent payable monthly, interest only (that is, $7,500 per month)

Tax-Structured Deal

Price: $1,050,000

Down: $50,000

Five-year note: $1,000,000 bearing interest at 13 percent with $200,000 payable at closing to be applied proportionately during the term to the interest accruing, with all other interest payable in monthly installments of $7,500

The two transactions are economically identical. Both require $250,000 at the closing. Both require monthly payments of $7,500. The difference is that there is only $50,000 in iceberg equity in the second deal; $200,000 is being written off over the next five years. If the term were shortened to four years, the interest rate would increase to 14 percent and the writeoffs would increase to $50,000 per year. You can see these calculations in three steps:

$$\$200,000 \div 4 = \$50,000$$
$$\$50,000 \div \$1,000,000 = .05$$
$$.09 + .05 = .14$$

This demonstrates one important principle in tax planning using prepaid interest: *Shorter maturities generate larger amounts of annual deductions.*

Another principle is also shown by each of our examples. Notice that even though we have prepaid the same $200,000 in all cases, the interest rate goes up when the term of the note grows shorter. When the notes had a five-year maturity, the rates were 4 percent (the zero-rate case) and 13 percent (the 9 percent case). When we shortened the maturity to four years, the rates increased to 5 percent and 14 percent, respectively. This is another principle: *Shorter maturities generate larger interest rates.*

In each of our examples, our seller was carrying a note for $1 million, or 80 percent of the purchase price. Since that might seem unrealistic too, let's assume that there's an institutional lender holding a $600,000 first-position note that bears interest at 9 percent per annum, payable interest only for fifteen years, and that the seller is willing to carry a $400,000 second payable interest only monthly for five years at the same 9 percent per annum rate.

Since our seller is only financing $400,000, our tax structured terms will change. If we desire the same $200,000 in prepaid interest, the new rate would be calculated using our soft dollar two-step:

$$\$200,000 \div 5 = \$40,000$$
$$\$40,000 \div \$400,000 = .10$$

With the third step, we see that the rate must be 19 percent. Our new terms are:

Price:	$1,050,000
Down:	$50,000
Fifteen-year note:	$600,000 bearing interest at 9 percent, payable interest only monthly
Five-year note:	$400,000 bearing interest at 19 percent with $200,000 payable at closing to be applied proportionately during the term to the interest accruing, with all other interest payable in monthly installments of $3,000 ($400,000 × 9 percent = $36,000 per year = $3,000 per month)

When we try to apply large portions of our former down payment to prepaid interest on purchase money notes that represent a smaller portion of the purchase price, the interest rate is increased dramatically. A rate of 19 percent may seem very high, and there are those who are fearful that this rate is so high that it will attract the attention of the IRS. These days, that's hardly true, for a number of reasons.

First, whether 19 percent is unusually high is a function of the marketplace at the time the loan is made. Since the prime (or reference or base) rate[6] has reached over 20 percent in the recent past, and since most credit cards still charge rates in the high teens, such rates aren't unusual anymore.

Second, the relevant market for determining interest rates for seller financing is the market in which lenders make second-, third-, and fourth-position loans and the owner has a minimum of equity. Lenders who make such loans are referred to as "hard money lenders." It is not uncommon for hard money lenders to charge five to fifteen or twenty points for making a loan and to set their interest rates in the high teens, even when conventional loans are far less expensive.

Finally, the IRS is often hard-pressed to recharacterize transactions when the paperwork is done right. This means having a properly drafted note reflecting the 19 percent rate. Some people draft notes with an interest rate of 9 percent, as in our example, and then state in the escrow instructions that $200,000 is being paid as prepaid interest. This won't work. The note doesn't contain terms that require the prepaid interest, and the IRS can have a field day. The paperwork doesn't support the taxpayer's view of the transaction and, even more important, there is no interest accrued to be prepaid. Although the burden is on the taxpayer to prove the availability of the deductions taken, the presentation of the proper documents shifts the burden to the IRS. Now you know why people pay their lawyers to write contracts and notes.

Now for the sophisticated stuff. In our previous examples, we prepaid interest for the entire term of the note. Naturally, we could get larger deductions each year if the prepaid interest were spread over fewer years. In order to do this, we'll have to specify a period shorter than the note's maturity. Doing that will require that we use something called a dual interest rate.

In our example, the seller wants a price of $1,250,000 with $250,000 down. There's a $600,000 first and the seller will carry $400,000. As before, if we wanted to prepay $200,000 and amortize this over the five-year second-position note, the rate would be 13 percent. We'd have $40,000 in deductions each year for five years.

We'll use dual rates to do better. A dual interest rate involves one interest rate at the commencement of the term and other rates at subsequent times. They are used by sellers in "creative financing" to motivate buyers to purchase their property. Usually they are developed in negotiation along these lines:

SELLER: I'll carry a $400,000 note for five years but I want to earn 9 percent.

BUYER: But if I pay 9 percent interest monthly, the property will lose too much money.

SELLER: OK. For the first two and one-half years, I'll collect 6 percent, but for the next two and one-half years, I want 12 percent. You can afford to pay 12 percent, since the property will be generating more income by then.

BUYER: OK (thinking that the property will be sold or refinanced by then anyway).

Let's see how we'd calculate and write the dual interest rate. We begin with 6 percent for the first two and one-half years and, of course, 12 percent for the last two and one-half years. To find the interest rate for the first two and one-half years assuming $200,000 in prepaid interest, we work with our three-step formula:

$$\$200,000 \div 2.5 = \$80,000$$
$$\$80,000 \div \$400,000 = .20$$
$$.06 + .20 = .26$$

Even if the early rate is high (in this case, 26 percent), it can be justified. The seller would want a high rate in the early years in the hope that the loan would be refinanced (because it's too expensive for the buyer) and the buyer would argue for a rate reduction in later years for the same reason.

Nevertheless, 26 percent is a high figure indeed. While the problem can be solved with an all-inclusive, you'll have to wait until the end of the chapter to find out how. For now, recognize that what we've done is assume that the note term has been shortened to the period during which the interest rate was low. The result is that the rate will be 26 percent for the first two and one-half years and 12 percent for the final two and one-half years.

More specifically, we'd draft our note to say: "For value received, the undersigned promises to pay seller the sum of $400,000 with interest thereon at the rate of 26 percent per annum proportionately to the interest accruing during the first two and one-half years of the term and 12 percent thereafter. Monthly installments during the term hereof in the sum of $2,000 shall be payable on the same day of each month commencing thirty days after the date hereof and continuing for two and one-half years and shall increase to $4,000 per month thereafter until maturity. Said payment shall be applied to all unpaid interest accrued since the last monthly payment."

It is also important to observe that these provisions not only provide for the payment of the interest, but also describe how it is to be applied to accrued interest. If there is no such provision, the IRS may attack the deduction for prepaid interest by claiming that it applies to the last interest to be accrued.

Naturally, all of this works just as well when you want to select an interest rate and find out how much prepaid interest will be generated. First, determine how much of an increase we're willing to create as a result of our prepayment of interest. This is the difference between the amount of interest charged at the higher rate on the dual interest note and the lower rate. In our example, the higher rate was 12 percent and the lower rate was 6 percent, a difference of 6 percent. Next, calculate the number of years of interest we are prepaying. This is the number of years to which the parties have agreed to the lower rate; in our example, two and one-half years. Finally, we multiply the difference in the rate by the number of years and then multiply this by the principal balance of the note. This will tell us how much money must be prepaid in order for the interest paid to raise the rate for the first two and one-half years to 12 percent. Following these steps, we'd have:

$$.12 - .06 = .06$$
$$.06 \times 2.5 = .15$$
$$.15 \times \$400,000 = \$60,000$$

Using this example, we have discovered that we could build in $60,000 in prepaid interest and keep the note interest rate at 12 percent throughout the entire five-year term. Of course, the note must be drafted to provide that the interest rate is 12 percent but that $60,000 is to be applied ratably to the interest being accrued and not paid by the monthly installments during the first two and one-half years. If we still want $200,000 in soft dollars, we have to turn to our cookbook for other techniques to handle the other $140,000.

Before we leave this chapter, however, let's see what might generate more soft dollars and handle the problem of the 26 percent rate that popped up in the first dual interest example. In that example, we were working with the seller's $400,000 second-position note. If we were to employ a wraparound note for $1 million, we might have an easier time. Since the $600,000 first and the $400,000 second are payable in monthly installments of interest only, it is easy to design a wraparound loan that is equivalent to them.

Let's not go to the extreme of handling the entire $200,000 as prepaid interest. Let's try $150,000. Remember, our starting point is 6 percent for the first two and one-half years and 12 percent for the second two and one-half years. That's the dual rate agreement. To embellish this as a result of prepaid interest, we take the same three steps as before:

$$\$150,000 \div 2.5 = \$60,000$$
$$\$60,000 \div \$1,000,000 = .06$$
$$.06 + .06 = .12$$

There. That's a little better. The wraparound format allows us to achieve an ideal situation. We have a 12 percent rate for the entire five-year term, and we've eliminated the glaringly high rate during the early years. Now we need to turn to our other techniques to handle another $50,000.

As you can see, the wraparound is a powerful device. With it, we can generate larger amounts of prepaid interest without changing the monthly payments, and without significantly distorting the interest rate on the note. Because of the ease with which wraparounds can be used to justify a greater number of points (see Chapter 9), and the impact on the rate in the course of designing prepaid interest, the wraparound is probably the most powerful and versatile of all the ingredients in our cookbook.[7]

After all this, you can see why the final ingredient is one of the best.

Ingredient 9:   Prepay interest.

NOTES

1. Internal Revenue Code Section 163(d) limits the deductibility of interest on funds borrowed to acquire or carry investment assets. If someone invests in a partnership that will own real estate, the rule won't apply unless the property is subject to a "net lease" as defined in Section 163(d)(4)(A). It does not affect the deductibility of mortgage interest.

2. A note having such terms might read as follows:

"I promise to pay to Lender the sum of $100,000 with interest thereon at the rate of 12 percent per annum from date [that is, the day the money is loaned]. Interest shall be payable in monthly installments in each calendar year hereafter, on the day and month this note is given. The entire principal balance, together with all accrued and unpaid interest thereon, shall be due and payable five years from date."

3. Institutional lenders have recently developed some very complex forms of amortizing loans, involving changes in interest rates, monthly payments of less than interest only, or negative amortization, where the principal balance increases as a result of changes in the interest rate. The variable- or adjustable-rate mortgages are designed to change some of the principles described in this chapter. However, these changes are irrelevant for our purposes because of our focus on seller financing.

4. A note requiring payment in advance, instead of in arrears, would be worded slightly differently than the note in note 2:

"I promise to pay to Lender the sum of $100,000 with interest thereon at the rate of 12 percent per annum from date. Interest shall be payable in annual installments in advance at the beginning of each calendar year on the day and month this note is given, commencing on the execution of this note. The entire principal balance, together with all unpaid interest, shall be due and payable five years from date."

5. We'll demonstrate the benefit of allowing taxpayers to accrue deductions by the following (which you're no longer allowed to do): Let's say a taxpayer becomes a 10 percent partner in a partnership that reports income using the accrual method. A 10 percent partner shares in 10 percent of each item of expense and income. If the partnership has a loan for $1 million with 12 percent interest, it accrues $120,000 in interest deductions each year. The partnership could deduct $120,000 whether or not it pays any money. If the terms of the loan do not require payment, the partner gets to deduct 10 percent of $120,000, or $12,000, without paying any cash. Some tax shelter promoters would establish accrual method partnerships and, using various methods of accounting, be able to pass on deductions of as much as $500,000 interest on the same $1 million loan described above.

6. The term "prime" has lost its former meaning. It used to mean the lowest rate available to a bank's most creditworthy borrower. Today it is simply an arbitrary benchmark. Many financial institutions have changed the name of their "prime" rate to get away from the old definition. Many banks now announce their benchmark rate—which is the starting point for pricing loans above and below the benchmark—whenever the bank believes that a change is appropriate. See Chapter 9 of *How to Borrow Money Below Prime* by Nelson E. Brestoff (Simon and Schuster, 1985) for a more complete explanation.

7. Drafting a wraparound requires some thought. For example, if the buyer paid off the wraparound before the maturity, the seller would owe the buyer money because the seller has collected interest before it accrued. This problem can be solved by a clause barring prepayment. In some cases, special provisions will be needed to insure that prepayment is possible by making an appropriate adjustment to account for the prepaid interest. In addition, instead of allocating the prepaid interest over a specified term (that is, the early years), the

maturity might be shortened (in the examples, to two and one-half years) with the buyer/borrower being given the right to extend the due date for another two and one-half years. Finally, it should be noted that underlying notes with amortization or more complicated interest provisions require careful calculations and drafting. More complicated terms, however, present no conceptual differences from the interest-only examples used in the text.

11

Seller's Side of the Beachball

I'm holding up a beachball, the kind with different colors in stripes. If I ask you what colors there are, you'll most likely tell me what colors *you* see. Since I might have different colors on my side of the beachball, I might disagree. Then it's a fight to see who's right and we tend to dig in. Since we have different perspectives, however, we might both be right. We'd each be better off if we walked around to the other side and stood in the other fellow's moccasins.

Let's go around the table and look at soft dollars from the seller's perspective. Tax structuring a deal involves tradeoffs that have to be negotiated. The deal points that I'm describing in this book are sometimes double-edged swords.

The double edge applies to sellers who deal with real estate infrequently, because they're truly *investors.* Investors can take advantage of several things: depreciation, the ability to exchange (instead of merely buying and selling), and long-term capital gains treatment. Investors, when they sell, are particularly fond of having their gains treated as long-term capital gains, and it is quite difficult to build in soft dollars. Some simply won't hear of it. Why? Because for each soft dollar they accept, an expense for us, they're getting income subject to tax *at ordinary income rates.* This is where the tradeoffs come in. In these situations, we'll have to pay a bit more in price to obtain the tax structuring we want.

For a whole group of sellers, however, *this isn't true.* There are a whole group of sophisticated sellers who can and will accept soft dollars without exacting any penalty from their buyers. They can accept as many soft dollars as we can think to structure. Fortunately, these sellers are precisely the right kind of people. The sellers who can accept soft dollars are real estate developers, condominium converters, and others who do so many real estate deals that they're considered to be "in the business." They built that new home you want to buy, and they're building that apartment complex or office building that's just right for your investment portfolio or pension plan. In tax parlance, they're called "dealers" because they hold property primarily for resale.[1] Dealers can't take advantage of depreciation, exchanges, or capital gains treatment. Because all they can ever hope to achieve is ordinary income when they sell from their inventory, a soft dollar deal can readily be achieved.

But that's the next chapter. I'll cover dealers in the next chapter and I'm only mentioning the subject here to keep from disappointing you. Let's slow down a bit and look at a seller's tax position. An investor is someone who buys a piece of property for investment purposes (to hold and sell for a profit) and who holds it for at least six months plus one day before selling. The two requirements for a capital gain are (1) the disposition (sale or exchange) of a capital asset and (2) a holding period of at least six months.

A capital asset may be loosely defined as property held by a taxpayer for investment. It does not include inventory[2] or property (personal or real) used in a trade or business.[3]

If a seller qualifies for a capital gain, how is the tax figured? So many people misunderstand how this works that I'm going to explain it carefully here. A gain is the difference between the net selling price (purchase price less selling costs) and the *basis* of the property. "Basis" is a term of art. The basis of any property starts off being its cost or original purchase price. Over time, the basis *decreases* dollar for dollar with the amount of depreciation expense taken during the holding period. In general:

$$\text{Basis} = \text{Cost} - \text{Depreciation}$$
$$\text{and}$$
$$\text{Gain} = \text{Net Selling Price} - \text{Basis}$$

As you can see from the formulas above, there's another way to look at it. The taxable gain is also the net selling price minus original cost *plus* depreciation previously taken.

Gain = Net Selling Price − Basis = Net Selling Price − (Cost −
Depreciation) = Net Selling Price − Cost + Depreciation

That's step one. Step two is simple. Multiply the taxable gain
by 40 percent. Of the total taxable gain, only 40 percent is
actually taxed. Notice that this is *not* the tax *rate*. Only 40 percent of the gain is *subject* to tax.

The third step is to add the 40 percent portion which *is*
subject to tax to all of your other ordinary income for the year.
When you add it in with everything else, you eventually raise
your taxable ("adjusted") gross income, eventually to the point
where the maximum 50 percent rate applies.

All of these steps are necessary: (1) compute the gain, (2)
multiply by 40 percent, and (3) determine your individual tax
rate (or bracket) by calculating or estimating the effect of
adding the income in with everything else.

A misconception has cropped up because people often use a
shorthand approach. I've seen people figure the capital gain
rate as being the result of multiplying 40 percent by the
maximum tax bracket of 50 percent. If you do this, you come up
with 20 percent. This is the *maximum* number of dollars that
you would have to pay to your friendly IRS Service Center, all
other things being equal. In other words, if your gain is
$20,000, the maximum loss to the tax collector (ignoring state
taxes) is 20 percent of the gain, or $4,000.

But there is no such thing as a capital gain rate. The 20 percent
figure is a maximum *tax*. It's misleading for sellers to think
about a capital gain rate, because they ignore the effect of their
bracket. If you're solidly in the 50 percent bracket, of course,
then the 20 percent tax is going to apply.[4] If a seller's bracket is
25 percent (that is, the adjusted gross income—including the
gain—subject to tax is at least $24,600), the tax payable on a
$20,000 gain is only 10 percent, or $2,000.

Sellers who give up a portion of their capital gain in order to
accept soft dollars are accepting a dollar that's worth a little less
because it'll be taxed a little more. It could be subject to a
maximum 50 percent bite as ordinary income as opposed to a
maximum 20 percent using the capital gains treatment.

Does this mean that you'll never be able to negotiate a soft dollar deal with someone who's giving up a portion of his or her capital gain? Of course not. It just means that soft dollars are worth a premium. A buyer might have to pay as much as $1.30 for every soft dollar. That's a large markup, but it won't affect the purchase price by very much, because soft dollars are usually only the equivalent of the cash portion of the deal. If we're paying a 30 percent premium on 20 percent of the deal, the purchase price will only go up by 6 percent. Given the dramatic effect on a buyer's tax bill and investment yield, this might be a price well worth paying. The buyer may bid up the purchase price a little because of the favorable tax position he or she wants.

The investor-seller's own tax position will determine the premium. In some cases, for example, an investor-seller might be in a position to accept soft dollars with no difficulty. If an investor has had significant tax shelter from other investments and reverses or casualties that have more than offset any previous tax liability, there might be "tax loss carry-forwards," which could easily absorb some additional ordinary income. A tax loss can be carried over for one or more of *fifteen* taxable years.[5] A seller with tax loss carry-forwards can absorb some additional ordinary income without any additional tax bite. You just have to ask.

NOTES

1. IRC Section 1221(1) denies capital gains treatment to profits reaped from the sale of "property held primarily for sale to customers in the ordinary course of his trade or business." See *Malat* v. *Riddell*, 383 U.S. 569, 86 S.Ct. 1030 (1966), for an interpretation of the statutes holding that "primarily" means "of first importance" or "principally." See also *Municipal Bond Corporation* v. *Comm.*, 341 F. 2d 683 (8th Cir. 1965).

If resale is an owner's primary purpose, the result may be dealer status. In *McManus* v. *Comm.*, 583 F.2d 443 (9th Cir. 1978), the court listed a number of factors: the length of holding, the nature of the acquisition, the frequency of sales over time, the nature and extent of the taxpayer's business, the activity of the seller with respect to the property, and the extent and nature of the transactions involved. In *McManus,* the partnership was in the business of buying, developing, and selling property. When part of its holdings were sold, it reported gains as ordinary income. When the state condemned part of its holdings, the partnership sought capital gains treatment. The court ruled that the condemnation was the equivalent of a sale (as opposed to the involuntary conversion of investment property; held, a dealer); *see Heebner* v. *U.S.,* 280 F.2d 228 (3rd Cir. 1960) (owner/architect/president of building company bought land, arranged financing, constructed buildings and sold them; held, a dealer); *Moore* v. *Comm.,* 30 TC 1306 (1958) (taxpayer made improvements required by local ordinance before he sold; held, *not* a dealer).

2. See Internal Revenue Code section 1221(1).

3. See Internal Revenue Code section 1221(2).

4. I'm going to ignore the effect of having to calculate the alternative minimum tax. This is an important detail, but too much of a distraction for my purposes in this book.

5. Tax loss carry-backs and carry-forwards are found in Internal Revenue Code section 172(a) and section 172(b)(1)(A and B). There are exceptions for special cases in section 172(b)(1)(C)-(H).

12

Dealer's Advantage

Before we go on, let's review the effect of tax structuring.

1. The same cash is paid;

2. There are allocations of the purchase price to land, structure, and FF&E (three-year property like automobiles and light trucks and five-year property like computers, desks, and other equipment) to take better advantage of depreciation schedules and ITCs;

3. There are allocations to contracts calling for reasonable and specific services to be provided by the seller for the benefit of the buyer, or contracts restricting the seller from conduct that might hurt the buyer;

4. There is seller financing, perhaps in the form of an all-inclusive promissory note, with terms (such as points, higher rates for specified periods, prepaid interest, and prepayment privileges) that generate interest expenses.

The result of these stratagems is that:

- Although the same cash is paid, equity is down;
- The level of debt is normal;
- Leverage is up;
- Tax losses are up; and
- The bottom-line—yield (return on investment)—is up.

This looks so attractive that you're probably wondering why everybody isn't doing it. More sellers should be. I'm not suggesting that the deals be redone strictly to reduce taxes—that's tax evasion. My argument is based on the observation that, even though economic reality calls for it, people rarely articulate their intentions with the proper language and documentation. When the paperwork spells out features of a deal that the parties truly intend, that's tax planning.

This stuff isn't for buyers only. Sellers should pay close attention. By giving good terms to a potential buyer, a seller can do two things that every seller clearly wants to do: make a sale and make a profit. Builders and professionals who are "in the business" should welcome a tax-structured deal with open arms. For them, it doesn't matter at all that the profit is washing in as ordinary income. Since they can't take advantage of the capital gain approach, ordinary income is all they ever expect to have. Far too few sellers ever broach the subject, even when they know that they're dealers.

Who are the dealers? I'll answer that question in just a moment. However, there's an oddball case that we should handle first. There is a corporate structure that allows the shareholders to receive their proportionate share of profits and losses as if the corporation were a partnership. This is the S corporation (still commonly known as a "Sub S").

A Sub S is formed when, within the first thirty days after the articles of incorporation are filed, the corporation elects to be taxed in this way. Once the election is accepted by the IRS, profits and losses pass through to the shareholders just as if they were partners in a partnership. These shareholders *can* take advantage of a capital gain treatment because the gain retains its character during the pass-through. The Sub S is a tax-reporting, not a tax-paying entity. The taxes are paid by the shareholders when they file their individual returns.

For such Sub S sellers, a tax-structured deal is harder to structure, unless, of course, the buyer is willing to pay the price, or all of the shareholders can absorb some ordinary income.

So much for the Sub S. It's far more likely that you'll run into a corporate seller that is both a tax-reporting and a tax-paying entity. This is the normal case. The corporation receives the profits and pays tax accordingly. The shareholder doesn't receive a share of profits. Instead, shareholders receive dividends. Dividends are ordinary income to the shareholder, but, alas, not even an expense to the corporation. Dividends are simply a pay-out of after-tax profits.

In small, closely held corporations, the problem is that the shareholders-owners can't take advantage of the capital gain treatment because it doesn't pass through. The gain is just gain, and the corporation will pay a tax at corporate rates if there is any profit at the end of the year.[1] For the shareholders, dividends are always ordinary income, regardless of the fact that the dividends might have been made possible because of capital gain at the corporate level.

The capital gain is stuck in the corporate boardroom and can't get out (without dissolving the corporation). Thus, corporate real estate executives, when they are selling, should have far less resistance to receiving a portion of the purchase price as ordinary income. The real sellers, the shareholders, can't take advantage of the capital gain anyway.

The next category of sellers is by far the largest group of sellers you'll meet: the "dealers." The phrase "dealer" is a technical one. Being in the real estate business can turn a real estate operator into a dealer, as far as the tax laws are concerned, in just the same way that a car lot operator is a dealer. Let's talk about selling cars for a moment and you'll see the point. Since we're now in the car business, selling retail, we'll have to buy some inventory for the lot. People will shop and buy. When they do, we'll sell some inventory and buy some more. That's busy-ness: frequent inventory turnover with a little profit, we hope, on each sale.

Now, back to real estate. Real estate developers, condominium converters, and sellers of single-family tracts all have inventory too: their unsold buildings, houses, condos and co-ops. When they sell their inventory, they look for the next venture or tract. Because they're considered to be "in the business" when their level of buying and selling reaches a certain point, they are "dealers." Once they achieve this status (it's something investors must scrupulously avoid), all gain is treated as ordinary income, and the capital gain approach is unavailable.[2] Anyone with dealer status is selling inventory; anyone selling inventory is limited to receiving ordinary income.

The distinction between an investor and a dealer has been the continuing source of controversy because of the tax consequences. An investor is a passive owner looking for future appreciation or holding property to generate cash flow (in which case the property is an asset used in a trade or business).[3] A dealer is someone who holds property with the primary intention of selling it to customers.

The case of the builder or developer is simple. They're dealers. The case is more difficult when an investor subdivides a piece of property in order to increase its value. Where once there was one, now there are many. The classic cases are the land subdivisions and the conversion of apartment buildings to condominium complexes. In each case, the courts will look at a number of factors, the most important of which is whether the conduct involved betokens a motive or intent to sell to customers in the ordinary course of business.[4]

This battle should not distract us. We're looking for sellers who know they're dealers. In general, they're not hard to find, because they've made a conscious decision to hold property as inventory for sale to the public. Such sales efforts are easy to find in every real estate section of every newspaper in the country. Most developers are, in fact, paying for the advertising to let you know who they are and what they have to sell, retail.[5]

So here's a very practical use for our new skill at building soft dollars into our acquisitions. If you're thinking of buying a home or condominium, buy from a developer. If you buy on the resale market, you'll run into investors.[6] If you approach a developer, you're approaching someone who will gladly tax-structure the deal.

There are no losers here. The buyer should be structuring his or her affairs to pay the least amount of tax, which all taxpayers are entitled to do. And the developer-seller is paving the way to a sale by cooperating in the structure of the transaction.

NOTES

1. A capital gain achieved by a corporation may be subject to taxation at a reduced rate using an alternative approach allowed by Internal Revenue Code section 1201(a). The rate is

28 percent, but may not be helpful if the corporation's ordinary income is less than $50,000 or in certain other circumstances. See Faggen, Ivan, et al. (Arthur Andersen & Co.), *Federal Taxes Affecting Real Estate,* Section 6.01(3) (Matthew Bender, 1984) (hereinafter cited as Arthur Andersen & Co., *Federal Taxes Affecting Real Estate).*

2. The taxpayer in *Culley* found that his real estate license was used against him. *Culley,* 29 TC 1076 (1958) (held, a dealer); but not having a real estate license doesn't prevent someone from being recast into the dealer's position. *Gault* v. *Comm.,* 332 F.2d 94 (1964) (held, a dealer). *See Mitchell,* 47 TC 120 (1966) (avoided dealer status by proving not in the business of selling real estate; held, not a dealer). However, if someone acting on the taxpayer's behalf buys the property and subdivides it, dealer status might be imputed to the taxpayer. *Brown* v. *Comm.,* 448 F.2d 514 (1971); *Boyer,* 58 TC 316 (1972) (held, a dealer). A partner in a joint venture with dealer status may become a dealer as to that property. *Brady,* J. Roland, 25 TC 682 (1956) (held, a dealer). *See Rockwell* v. *Comm.,* 512 F.2d 822 (1975) (large fraction of taxpayer's income from sales of real estate; held, a dealer); *Glover,* 55,329 P-H Memo TC (1955) (taxpayer stated he was a dealer in his tax return; held, a dealer).

3. Internal Revenue Code section 1231(b)(1)(b).

4. Generally, see Arthur Andersen & Co., *Federal Taxes Affecting Real Estate,* Chapter 10; Taylor, "Dealers and Investors in Real Estate," 7 *Journal of Real Estate Taxation* 395 (1980) (mathematical analysis of 108 tax court decisions from 1960 to 1977). *See also Chandler* v. *U.S.,* 226 F.2d 403 (1955) (a land trust sold 536 parcels of land over a nine-year period, but was nevertheless not a dealer because the original parcel, over a million acres, was so large that the court held that there was no choice but to subdivide; held, not a dealer); *Smith* v. *Dunn,* 224 F.2d 353 (1955) (taxpayer who inherited land, subdivided it, and sold the lots was not a dealer because he did not acquire the land on his own initiative for resale purposes; held, not a dealer); *Ayling,* 32 TC No. 59 (taxpayer sold thirteen lots in four years with deed restrictions preventing low-priced homes in order to protect the value of his own home; held, not a

dealer); *Dillon* v. *Comm.*, 213 F.2d 218 (1955) ("changed conditions" supported investor intent at time of acquisition; held, not a dealer).

5. *Tidewell* v. *Comm.*, 298 F.2d 864 (1962) (advertising; held, a dealer); *Municipal Bond Corp.* v. *Comm.*, 341 F.2d 683 (1965) (rental property listed with agent, use of "for sale" signs and advertising; held, not a dealer); *Gates,* 52 TC 898 (1969) (lack of advertising did not prevent finding of dealer status in seller's market; held, a dealer); *Starke* v. *Comm.*, 312 F.2d 608 (1963) (unsolicited offer; held, not a dealer); *Au* v. *U.S.*, 53 AFTR 2d 84-999 (1984) (in a loss situation, the taxpayer sought dealer status in order to obtain ordinary loss writeoffs; because the property was originally intended for development as a shopping center and held for profit, the use of a realtor was not enough to convert the taxpayer into someone holding primarily for sale to customers in the ordinary course of business; held, not a dealer—a victory for the IRS because of the limitations on deducting capital losses).

6. A developer can have a dual capacity and hold certain property for investment purposes. In general, such property has to be different in nature from the property he or she deals in as a business (For example, residential as a business; commercial for investment). *William B. Daugherty,* 78 TC 623 (1982); *Maddux Construction Co.,* 54 TC 1278 (1970); *Oace,* 39 TC 743 (1963); *Howell,* 57 TC 546 (1972); *Westchester Development Co.,* 63 TC 198 (1978); *Casalina Corp.,* 60 TC 694 (1973); *Biedermann,* 68 TC 1 (1977); *Pritchett,* 63 TC 149 (1974).

13

For New Home Buyers Only: A Case Study

Let's see what we can do with these principles when it comes to buying a home.

For most people, buying a home is a major, long-term financial decision. It's one of the largest purchases most people ever make.

Yet while buying a home may be the heart of the American Dream, only one of our nine ingredients can be used to our advantage here. Since we can't depreciate our own homes, there's really no point to allocations. Since there's usually no trade or business associated with owning the homes in which we live, there's no reason to forge consulting or other agreements and there's no opportunity for an investment tax credit. Of course, homes can be depreciated if used in part for business. If you know in advance that you'll have an office at home, then allocations are important when negotiating the purchase.

The good news is, however, that one of the most powerful ingredients—the deductibility of interest—is still available to us. Everything we discussed in connection with purchase money notes still applies. Further, because the availability of favorable financing of a new home is such a major consideration for developers, who primarily want sales results, our earlier discussion has even greater effect. The sellers you'll want to buy from when you buy your first home are precisely the people who should be happy to structure the financing to suit you.

And now for the really good news: When you're buying your home, all reasonable points that you might pay can be written off *in the first year*.[1] To clearly illustrate, let's not complicate the case by using prepaid interest, although you'd certainly want to structure some in an actual purchase.

Let's see how this might work. For tax purposes, interest is deductible if you itemize using Schedule A (see Figure 13-1). There are certain hurdles for taxpayers to cross before the total Schedule A deductions mean anything. The highest hurdle, however, is $3,400 for a husband and wife filing a joint return.[2] Since home ownership involves both mortgage interest and property taxes, which are also deductible on Schedule A, the purchase of a home will usually make it worthwhile to itemize.

There are other categories, of course, on Schedule A. Deductions are allowed for medical expense, state, local, sales, real estate and other taxes, charitable contributions, tax return preparation fees, and miscellaneous items. For purposes of illustration, we'll assume that these other Schedule A deductions add up to $3,400, the highest threshold. Every dollar of interest on a home mortgage, whether payable to a financial institution or to an individual, will be deductible.

How is it that people usually buy their homes? In the usual case, they pay 10 or 20 percent as a cash down payment, because the developer (or buyer) has arranged financing from a bank or savings and loan for an 80 or 90 percent mortgage.

In recent years, however, high interest rates have forced developers into new approaches. Instead of being cashed out, the design has been to blend the high mortgage financing costs with the lower rates offered on the seller financing to achieve an overall result that is more affordable.

In my opinion, developers should be doing this as a matter of standard operating procedure. The presence in the marketplace of seller financing by builders and developers ought to trigger the use of all-inclusive notes, points, and prepaid interest. For example, the developer could arrange an 80 to 90 percent mortgage and offer to take back paper. Assuming that we can convince the institutional lender to go forward even though we, as buyers, aren't plunking very much down, we have an opportunity for some tax structuring. This may require a strong relationship between the institutional lender and the developer (or a desperate lender). If there are no problems with the underlying financing (that is, the lender requirements

Figure 13-1.

SCHEDULES A&B (Form 1040)	Schedule A—Itemized Deductions	OMB No. 1545-0074
Department of the Treasury Internal Revenue Service (O)	(Schedule B is on back) ► Attach to Form 1040. ► See Instructions for Schedules A and B (Form 1040).	19**84** 07

Name(s) as shown on Form 1040 | Your social security number

Medical and Dental Expenses
(Do not include expenses reimbursed or paid by others.)
(See Instructions on page 19)

1 Prescription medicines and drugs; and insulin . . . . . | 1
2 a Doctors, dentists, nurses, hospitals, insurance premiums you paid for medical and dental care, etc. . . . . | 2a
b Transportation and lodging . . . . | 2b
c Other (list—include hearing aids, dentures, eyeglasses, etc.) ► .... | 2c
3 Add lines 1 through 2c, and write the total here . . . | 3
4 Multiply the amount on Form 1040, line 33, by 5% (.05) . | 4
5 Subtract line 4 from line 3. If zero or less, write -0-. **Total** medical and dental . ► | 5

Taxes You Paid
(See Instructions on page 20)

6 State and local income taxes . . . . | 6
7 Real estate taxes . . . . | 7
8 a General sales tax (see sales tax tables in instruction booklet) | 8a
b General sales tax on motor vehicles . . . . . | 8b
9 Other taxes (list—include personal property taxes) ► .... | 9
10 Add the amounts on lines 6 through 9. Write the total here. **Total** taxes . ► | 10

Interest You Paid
(See Instructions on page 20)

11 a Home mortgage interest you paid to financial institutions . | 11a
b Home mortgage interest you paid to individuals (show that person's name and address) ► .... | 11b
12 Total credit card and charge account interest you paid . . . . | 12
13 Other interest you paid (list) ► .... | 13
14 Add the amounts on lines 11a through 13. Write the total here. **Total** interest . ► | 14

Contributions You Made
(See Instructions on page 20)

15 a Cash contributions. (If you gave $3,000 or more to any one organization, report those contributions on line 15b.) . . . | 15a
b Cash contributions totaling $3,000 or more to any one organization. (Show to whom you gave and how much you gave.) ► .... | 15b
16 Other than cash (attach required statement) . . . . . | 16
17 Carryover from prior year . . . . | 17
18 Add the amounts on lines 15a through 17. Write the total here. **Total** contributions . ► | 18

Casualty and Theft Losses

19 Total casualty or theft loss(es). (You must attach Form 4684 or similar statement.) (see page 21 of Instructions) . . . . ► | 19

Miscellaneous Deductions
(See Instructions on page 21)

20 Union and professional dues . . . . | 20
21 Tax return preparation fee . . . . | 21
22 Other (list type and amount) ► .... | 22
23 Add the amounts on lines 20 through 22. Write the total here. **Total** miscellaneous . ► | 23

Summary of Itemized Deductions
(See Instructions on page 22)

24 Add the amounts on lines 5, 10, 14, 18, 19, and 23. Write your answer here. | 24
25 If you checked Form 1040 { Filing Status box 2 or 5, write $3,400 } { Filing Status box 1 or 4, write $2,300 } { Filing Status box 3, write $1,700 } . . . . | 25
26 Subtract line 25 from line 24. Write your answer here and on Form 1040, line 34a. (If line 25 is more than line 24, see the Instructions for line 26 on page 22.) . . . . ► | 26

For Paperwork Reduction Act Notice, see Form 1040 Instructions.   Schedule A (Form 1040) 1984 for cash down or specific loan-to-value ratios), then we can create our "nothing down" $95,000 all-inclusive transaction with 5.25 points and completely write off the cash paid out.

However, when a lender imposes a down payment requirement, or insists on loan-to-value ratios, we can't pay less down, reduce the price, and pay the difference in points as we discussed in Chapter 9. By reducing the price (assumed by many appraisers to equal the market value), we'd be reducing the loan the lender would be willing to make, and the deal would never be made.

We have to do something else. In such cases, we have to negotiate differently. Instead of points, we consider building in a prepayment penalty while adjusting the interest rate on the note. In effect, we're going to fund what would otherwise have been the down payment in the first or second year *after* the sale.

Prepayment penalties are considered payments for the use or forbearance of money. Thus, they are deductible as interest.[3] Taxpayers cannot, however, deduct interest prepaid beyond the current taxable year. Such interest must be capitalized and deducted (in effect, amortized) over the life of the loan.[4]

Thus, there are three things to build in: a provision for a prepayment penalty, an interest rate, and the term of the note.

In accordance with a well-known industry custom, we'll work with a prepayment penalty equal to six months of unearned interest. Lenders charge such penalties because they've lost the opportunity to earn future interest on the loan that's been repaid and because they theoretically have the costs involved in placing the money with another borrower. Practically speaking, the other borrower usually pays points just to get the loan. If the money turnaround is rapid, the lender will be paid twice. If the money can't be readily placed, then there may well be "warehousing" costs, which means that the money will earn only bank interest instead of the higher returns desired. This justifies the prepayment penalty.

Let's continue to work with our $100,000 figure, as in Chapter 9. Instead of a duplex, however, we'll buy a single-family home from a developer. We'll assume an $80,000 first mortgage from a bank or savings and loan, which is, in turn, wrapped by a $100,000 all-inclusive in favor of the developer. We've paid nothing down.

The developer, however, wants to be cashed out. If we can get the $20,000 equity in the note to him or her soon enough, the wait will be worthwhile. After all, the developer has a sale, and the sale has resulted in a payment of $80,000 by the new institutional long-term lender. That money either reduces the developer's construction loan—which reduces both risk and interest expense—or, if the construction loan has already been repaid, gets banked by the developer.

Now, how about that $20,000? We have to work backward to determine the interest rate we need so that the prepayment of this $20,000 will be mostly interest.

Let's not be greedy. Suppose we'd be happy deducting approximately half of what would otherwise have been our $20,000 down payment. We need a prepayment penalty, therefore, of $10,000. Since the developer isn't going to pay our first mortgage for us, the interest rate on this all-inclusive needs to be a combination of the rate on the first mortgage and a rate that will generate a sufficiently large prepayment penalty.

In this case, let's assume that the interest rate on the $80,000 first mortgage is 13 percent. For an all-inclusive of $100,000, then, we'd need an interest rate of 20 percent in order to generate a six-month prepayment penalty of $10,000 ($100,000 × 20 percent = $20,000 annually = $10,000 for six months). The term of the all-inclusive will be three years even though we plan to pay it off in the first year. After all, we have a strong incentive to prepay the all-inclusive because it now carries such a high rate. Interest would be payable monthly in an amount that would cover the amount due on the first mortgage, and the balance would accrue without further interest, with the principal due at maturity (in three years). Since a thirty-year amortization at 13 percent on the $80,000 first mortgage results in monthly payments of $884.96 (annually, $10,619.52), the interest payable monthly by the buyer on the $100,000 must be roughly 11 percent (annually, $11,000; monthly, $916.67), enough to cover the payment due on the first. The balance of 9 percent would accrue.

Because of these terms, we'd owe $20,000 in interest during the first year, but pay only $11,000. Some time during the first few months of the year, however, we'd offer the $20,000 in unpaid principal (the difference between the $100,000 all-inclusive note and the $80,000 first mortgage) to the developer. The prepayment penalty is fixed by these terms, however, at $10,000 (six months' worth of interest on $100,000 at 20 percent).

Now, while the developer-seller is willing to take paper for such high rates for a moderate amount of time, getting cash as soon as possible is the real goal. The prospect of paying 20 percent per annum is the stick; a discount on the amount necessary for an early payoff is the carrot.

In our contrived example, a deep discount was offered as an incentive in the terms of the all-inclusive note as originally written. The discount provision was that the $20,000 owed would be discounted to $10,000 if paid during the first year, $15,000 if paid during the second year, and not at all if paid during the third year.

With a carrot and stick approach like this, however, you have to be pretty confident about being able to come up with the necessary $20,000 during the first year to pay the discounted principal of $10,000 and the prepayment penalty of $10,000. If you can't follow through, the interest expense keeps going at a high rate and the discount is lower. In the third year, the interest expense would be very high with no discount whatever.

While this may seem a scary prospect, it is precisely this provision that turns the carrot and stick provision into one of real substance. A payoff in the second or third years is really something to avoid.

Generally speaking, though, you shouldn't worry. Normally you wouldn't go shopping for a house unless you had the money necessary for a normal down payment anyway. I'm assuming, therefore, that you have the money. We're simply using our cash more intelligently in the meantime.

The result of structuring the deal this way, of course, is to reduce the equity from $20,000 to $10,000, and to increase the deductible interest expense in the first year by $10,000. The $10,000 is deductible in the first year because the all-inclusive has been repaid during that time. Its term is up. Since the interest paid, including prepayment penalty, is amortized over the short—*and controllable*—life of the note, all of the expense is a first year writeoff.

In our hypothetical example, we've paid the developer

$20,000 during the first year after the closing. In order to take account of the developer's forgone interest (he would have been able to earn interest on the money had it been received at the closing), a little extra could be built in. This can be done by decreasing the discount a bit, increasing the interest rate slightly, or tacking on a fee for preparing and processing the reconveyance necessary to eliminate the paid-off all-inclusive from the record. For the buyer, this would be a small transaction cost for a favorably structured deal. If the all-inclusive is paid off promptly after the deal closes escrow, the buyer will have paid $20,000 and a very little bit more to cover forgone interest, and will be left with a perfectly standard $80,000 first mortgage. The developer will be happily cashed out. Your equity will be cut in half and your Schedule A deductions increased by $10,000. A cash payment of $20,000 was made, but $10,000 was paid in deductible soft dollars.

Is the paperwork for this structuring very complex? Not at all. In any seller-financed transaction, there's a note due to the seller. In addition to the note, there's a document making the property security for that note (the mortgage or deed of trust). In any payoff, there's a reconveyance. All of these documents, including all-inclusive notes and all-inclusive deeds of trust, have been reduced to printed forms by title companies and others because they write themselves into the form as the trustee (hoping to pick up the trustee's fees in the event of a foreclosure or the reconveyance fees in the event of a payoff).

So the paperwork is no mystery. In fact, it's routine. We simply have to modify the terms of the note to take advantage of the law. In fact, all we did was add a paragraph. Although a provision of the carrot and stick variety must be customized for each deal, one version, which I used in a recent transaction, is included below to give you an idea of how it's done. Notice, in the last sentence of the note's terms, that a loan origination fee (points) was added to the picture.

TERMS OF ALL-INCLUSIVE NOTE

Terms of All-Inclusive Note. The principal balance of the All-Inclusive Note shall be one million sixty-five thousand dollars ($1,065,000) with interest thereon payable at the rate of twenty percent (20%) per annum as follows: All monthly payments made prior to January 1, 1983, shall be in the amount of $7,661.77; thereafter the monthly payments shall be $17,750 until October 1, 1989, at which time the entire unpaid principal balance shall be due. Said All-Inclusive Note shall also provide a statement that in the event the Seller's total equity (in the amount of $155,000) is paid prior to December 31, 1982, Seller will lose the opportunity to earn a high rate of interest over the life of this All-Inclusive Note and, therefore, will charge a pre-payment penalty of $60,200 on the existing balance of said All-Inclusive Note. In the event of prepayment, seller agrees to fully reconvey the All-Inclusive Deed of Trust described by this Paragraph 1.4 and to cancel the All-Inclusive Note it secures. Purchaser further agrees to pay Seller the sum of $89,800 as a loan origination fee on the full amount of said All-Inclusive Deed of Trust at Close of Escrow.

NOTES

1. IRC section 461(g)(2).

2. For a married couple filing a joint return or a qualifying widow(er) with dependent children, the first $3,400 in Schedule A deductions are no benefit. For single or head of household taxpayers, the first $2,300 do not count. For married taxpayers filing separate returns, there is no benefit to the first $1,700 in deductions. See the Schedule A example in Figure 12-1.

3. Rev. Rul. 57-198, 1957-1 CB 94.

4. IRC section 461(g)(1).

14

Condos, *Sí*; Co-ops, *No*

The structuring I've gone through for a single-family home needs to be freed from a stereotype. Most of us think of a single-family home as a detached structure with a garage, a front yard, perhaps a pool in the back, and of course, neighbors on adjoining lots.

For tax purposes, however, the term "single-family residence" includes condominiums and co-ops. It doesn't matter that the units are attached, that the garage and pool are shared, or that the neighbors are above the ceiling, to either side, and below the floor.

There are some similarities and some differences with the conventional notion of a single-family home, however, when it comes to financing.

The simplest case is the condominium. Condominiums are popular throughout the world. In central areas, space becomes scarce, and people build up instead of out. The condominium therefore involves the exclusive ownership of airspace and the nonexclusive ownership of the common areas: the garage, recreational facilities and hallways.

From the financing point of view, the condominium is the equivalent of the single-family home. The reason is that the developer sells each unit separately for someone's exclusive use. Even though there are common areas associated with the whole project, the condominium home is a unit of inventory for the dealer-developer. New construction projects are not different from conversions of what once were apartments. The dealer-developer holds the units for resale in just the way I described in the preceding chapter.

Just as important, the financing is individualized. The developer may have a construction or rehabilitation loan that blankets the entire project. These interim loans are designed to be paid down by the sale of the individual units, which are then released from the lien of the blanket loans. The purchase of each unit is individually financed with a "permanent" lender, which takes back a new first-position loan on the unit alone. Of course, in a situation like this, the developer can take back a second or, as was suggested in the previous chapter, employ an all-inclusive. With individualized financing, condominium sales are identical to new tract housing deals.

Thus, instead of buying from the developer of a tract of new homes in an outlying area, you can buy into a condominium project in the heart of the city and get the same result. Unless the seller is involved in a very small project, say of eight units or less, and is holding the product for investment purposes, the seller knows that he, she, or it is a dealer. Because of that fact of life, you can structure a soft dollar deal without adversely affecting the seller in any way.

Co-ops, however, are different. In general, co-ops are corporations that own the whole project subject to an overall financial scheme. The problem is not that the developers aren't dealers. Dealers they are.

The problem is that the financing is not individualized. Each co-op owner lives in his or her unit by virtue of being a corporate shareholder with an appurtenant right to live in a certain unit. The money everyone pays into the corporation is pooled to make the monthly payments on a mortgage that encumbers the entire project. While the unit holders may not be personally obligated to the lender, the tradeoff is that individualized deal-making may be difficult.[1]

If the financing can be individualized, as in the case of the condominium, then a soft dollar deal has a chance. California recognized that people might want to finance their cooperative units separately from the blanket note owned by the corporation and the blanket deed of trust encumbering the property. The owner must assign his or her interest in the proprietary lease and the loan must have a term of thirty years or less, in substantially equal monthly installments, and not exceed 80 percent of the market value of the stock or membership certificates. The proprietary lease must also provide that there can be no sublease in excess of one year and that, in the event of a default, the bank may sell the stock without the prior consent of the corporation after giving thirty days' prior written notice to the borrower and the corporation.[2]

In California, condos *sí* and co-ops *sí*. For other states, ask your banker or lawyer.

NOTES

1. This aspect of the financing of co-ops is often overlooked. A pro rata share of a common mortgage cannot be refinanced to pull out iceberg equity, regardless of the reason. For example, co-op owners may not be able to use their equity for the education of their children or in case of emergencies.

2. Calif. Financial Code section 1236, added in 1977.

15

Master Class: Case Study for Investors

In this case study, we're going to take the principles we've learned and apply them to a real estate investment. In this case, we'll be dealing with a shopping center, but the application of the principles would be the same if we were dealing with an office building, an apartment complex, or any other kind of income-producing, depreciable real estate investment. In addition, the principles apply to the purchase of single-family homes so long as they're bought for income potential as investments. As opposed to the case of our principal residences, in this case all of the ingredients discussed earlier are available to us. We can really cook up a deal now.

By the way, all of the facts and figures in this example are from an actual transaction. I've changed the name and location, however, to protect an innocent property.

Meet Summerfield Center. Summerfield Center is a contemporary shopping center designed to service a suburban community and its immediately surrounding trade center of approximately 30,000 people. There are four first-class separate buildings with 48,000 square feet of space. Surrounding these buildings are grounds of 5.5 acres. The mall is anchored with strong tenants—a market, drugstore, hardware store, shoe store, computer store, fast food outlet, and the like. It's 97 percent leased.

Originally, the seller wanted $5,895,000 for Summerfield, with $1,500,000, a bit more than 25 percent, down.

As you'll see, we will reduce the purchase price from $5,895,000 to $4,590,000, and the down payment from

$1,500,000 to only $195,000. The wrap-around, or all-inclusive, will be for $4,395,000 ($4,590,000 − $195,000).

As you'll also see, we will still have to pay $1,500,000 at the closing in cash to our seller—$195,000 for the down payment and $1,305,000 for certain agreements and interest. There are five components to the cash paid at the closing. The first is the down payment ($195,000). Next, there's interest paid on the promissory note to be given by the seller. Third, our seller will guarantee the leases for one year. Fourth, a management company associated with the seller will provide supervisory and consulting services for two years. Finally, our seller will sign a covenant-not-to-compete in the immediate trade area (i.e., not to develop or operate a commercial shopping center for the next two years).

The particular numbers from this transaction may look a bit funny, but that is partly because the closing took place on May 1, 1984, with the result that there were only eight months in the first year. In addition, some of the numbers are the result of intense bargaining between the parties. So long as they are reasonably reflective of the marketplace, there can be little argument with such numbers. Besides, figures that neatly tie together look contrived. While we are clearly designing the transaction, part of the artistry of that design involves building in the appearance of *no design at all*.

Below, then, is shown the allocation of cash at the closing.

Down payment	$ 195,000
Interest	781,408
Lease guarantee	150,000
Supervisory mgmt. fee	223,592
Covenant-not-to-compete	150,000
Total	$1,500,000

Figure 15-1. Cash Paid.

Let's talk about some of these ingredients. The lease guarantee is for a year and is secured by the seller's all-inclusive note. As the payments fall due, any rent due but unpaid becomes an offset. In other words, if some tenant fails to pay in accordance with a lease, the payments due to the seller under the note will be reduced by the same amount. This is automatic insurance that the rent guarantee has teeth. No lawsuits needed, thank you.

The supervisory management agreement calls for a management company affiliated with the seller to provide supervisory and consulting services for two years. The contract is paid in advance at the closing. It's based on a percentage of the scheduled gross income.

The all-inclusive promissory note is much more complex, and we'll discuss it in more detail later. The terms, however, are as follows: $781,408 in interest is payable at the closing; monthly payments of $33,333 must be made for the first two years ($399,996 per year) and thereafter at the rate of $40,320.83 per month ($483,849.96 per year). No prepayment is allowed during the first two years, but after two years any interest actually paid is, to the extent it was not yet due, the basis for a prepayment penalty. In accordance with the industry custom, the prepayment penalty is equal to six months of unaccrued (not yet earned) interest. The dual interest rate schedule on the $4,395,000 of unpaid principal varies in accordance with the schedule below.

Year	Rate
1 (1984)	17.5%
2 (1985)	15.5%
3 (1986)	13.5%
4 (1987)	11.5%
Thereafter until maturity on April 1, 1990	10.542%

Figure 15-2.   Note Interest Rates.

Let's see how the prepaid interest was calculated. The terms require monthly payments during the first two years of $33,333. That's $399,996 per year. During years three and four, the monthly payment goes up to $40,320.83, or $483,850 per year (rounded). By applying the rate schedule to the note principal of $4,395,000, we can see how much interest is being prepaid during the first forty-eight months (see table on opposite page).

Now, because there are only eight months available to accrue interest in the first year, 1984, we can only count on two-thirds of the first year prepaid interest as a deduction in that year. The other four months' worth will show up in 1985. Similarly, we can deduct eight months' worth of the interest prepaid for the second year (months 13 through 24), and four months' worth of the interest prepaid for the third year, and so on. The actual deductions will fall into 1984, 1985, 1986, 1987, and 1988 as shown below (rounded).

Year	Rate (%)	Accrued	Payable	Prepaid
1	17.5	$ 769,125	$ 399,996	$369,129
2	15.5	681,225	399,996	281,229
3	13.5	593,325	483,850	109,475
4	11.5	505,425	483,850	21,575
Total		$2,549,100	$1,767,692	$781,408

1984[a]	1985[b]	1986[c]	1987[d]	1988[e]
$246,086	$310,529	$166,726	$50,875	$7,192

Total = $781,408

a. $369,129 × 8 / 12.
b. ($369,129 × 4 / 12) + ($281,229 × 8 / 12).
c. ($281,229 × 4 / 12) + ($109,475 × 8 / 12).
d. ($109,475 × 4 / 12) + ($21,575 × 8 / 12).
e. $21,575 × 4 / 12.

Oh, yes, the down payment. The down payment is something we can't write off. We *could* structure the transaction so that we'd pay nothing down. Since we don't believe in being piggish, we'll pay something down. The supervisory management fee is whatever we need to balance our other figures so that we'll be paying the agreed-upon amount of cash at the closing. Although the amount seems oddball, it reflects a reasonable percentage of the center's income. It also balances the other figures so that the total amount of cash paid at the closing will be equal to $1,500,000. The other numbers reflect an effort to obtain meaningful obligations from the seller at realistic prices. In this case, the down payment has been reduced to a bit over 4 percent of the tax-structured purchase price ($195,000 is 4.25 percent of $4,590,000). *That's* leverage.

Are we done? No. We have allocations to do. These are very easy, because most sellers with capital assets don't care how you pay for them. A seller seeking a capital gain treatment for land, real estate, and personal property will get it regardless of how much is paid for each (though recapture of accelerated depreciation and depreciation of personal property will result in ordinary income). A "dealer" also doesn't care because all of the gain will be ordinary income in his or her hands anyway.

As we discussed earlier, however, allocations make a significant difference to the buyer, because personal property can be depreciated over three or five years, whereas structures can be depreciated over eighteen years. Land, of course, can't be written off at all.

With the tax assessor's allocations as a guide, but only a guide, the buyer and seller reach agreement. The buyer will pay so much for land, so much for structure, and so much for the personal property. The schedule looked like the one below.

Land	$1,000,000
Personal Property,	
Signage & Decor	564,000
Structures	3,026,000
Total	$4,590,000

Figure 15-3.   Allocations of Purchase Price.

Now, remember, there are two additional benefits that attach to personal property: the investment tax credit and bonus depreciation. We'll see their impact later when we consider the "after-tax" yield to a 50 percent taxpayer.

Before we get too far ahead of ourselves, however, we need to see how the rules of depreciation operate on our allocations to personal property and structures. Then we'll summarize the tax losses for the last eight months of 1984, and all of 1985, 1986, and 1987.

The rules of depreciation are the ACRS schedules that I've spelled out in Chapter 6 and Appendix A. They apply to any situation.

In our case study, the ACRS schedule (using Appendix A, Table 3) looks like the one below.

	1984	1985	1986	1987
Personal Property	$ 93,060[a]	$253,800	$124,080	$ 93,060
Structures	112,074[b]	168,111	168,111	168,111
Totals	$205,134	$421,911	292,191	261,171

Figure 15-4.   Depreciation Schedule.

a. Note the use of the half year convention.

b. This is eight-twelfths of the annual deduction allowed by depreciating $3,026,000 over eighteen years ($3,026,000 ÷ 18 = $168,111).

Our next table will show the effect of all of these ingredients taken together. There are portions of the deductible expenses associated with each item in various years because of the amortization periods. In the case of the management agreement and covenant-not-to-compete, the amortization is two years. Because there were only eight months left in 1984, we had to allocate twelve months to 1985 and four months to 1986. Thus, 33.33 percent of the writeoff falls in 1984, 50 percent in 1985 and 16.67 percent in 1986. In the case of the lease guarantee (one year), you'll see that two-thirds of the expense is associated with the eight months of 1984 and one-third with the four months of 1985. The tax losses for 1984 through 1987 (a total of three years and eight months) can now be summarized in the table below.

	1984	1985	1986	1987
Interest	$246,086	$310,529	$166,726	$ 50,875
Lease guarantee	100,000	50,000	—	—
Mgmt. Agreem't	74,531	111,796	37,265	—
Covenant-not-to-compete	50,000	75,000	25,000	—
Depreciation (from Figure 15-4)	205,134	421,911	292,191	261,171
Totals	$675,751	$969,236	$521,182	$312,046
Estimated Benefit to 50 Percent Taxpayer	$337,875	$484,618	$260,591	$156,023

Figure 15-5.   Tax Losses.

We're still not done. I've forgotten to tell you that the property generated a positive cash flow from the very start because the amount of debt was manageable. This was the attraction in the first place. With an economic investment of over 25 percent ($1,500,000 paid down against a $5,895,000 economic price), the property's lease structure would, against normal operating expenses and debt service, generate cash flows of $156,957 in 1984, $190,550 in 1985, $177,633 in 1986, and $143,749 in 1987.

The first attraction was that positive cash flow of $156,957. Since we were investing $1,500,000, we could expect a first-year "cash on cash" return of slightly more than 10 percent. ($156, 957 ÷ $1,500,000 equals 10.4638 percent). We could have put our money in a money market savings account and done as well. Except, of course, that money in such a savings account has no tax structuring opportunities, no tax shelter and no possibility of further appreciation.

To see our results, we must add up all of the benefits that we've been able to design into our purchase. There are three: the tax benefits that are the end result of depreciation and our various ingredients; the investment tax credit associated with the personal property; and last, but not least, the cash flow. See the table below.

	1984	1985	1986	1987
Est. Tax Benefits	$337,875	$484,618	$260,591	$156,023
ITC	56,400	—	—	—
Cash Flow	156,957	190,550	177,633	143,749
Totals	$551,232	$675,168	$438,224	$299,772
Yield to 50 Percent Taxpayer	36.7%	45.0%	29.2%	20.0%

Figure 15-6.   Transaction Yield.

In other words, if we were in the 50 percent tax bracket, the return on our $1,500,000 in 1984 would be 36.7 percent, not 10.46 percent. We've improved our position by a factor of over 350 percent. By the end of 1986, after only two years and eight months, our benefits would be $1,664,624, and we will have received benefits of $164,624 *more* than our initial investment. Our capital will have been completely recovered in less than three years, which is a very rapid rate of recovery indeed. It's also true that, with tax structuring, we've turned an attractive, but normal, 10 percent cash-on-cash deal into a spectacular transaction. By the end of 1987, we'll have received $668,889 in cash, $56,400 in tax credits, and $1,239,107 in tax benefits (for a 50 percent taxpayer). This shelters not only the positive cash flow for this deal, but also $570,218 in ordinary income *from any other source* ($1,239,107 − $668,889 = $570,218), ignoring the ITC.

If I may be forgiven for the fair use of a famous advertising slogan, "This is the only way to fly."

16

The Midwives

While dealers are easy to get along with because all of their income is ordinary income, sellers with investor status are harder to convince. They're not excited about soft dollars. To them, soft dollars are completely unappetizing. Investors only want income that will be treated as long-term capital gain. In some cases, you might be willing to pay a premium to such a reluctant seller to build soft dollars into the deal. The price might be reasonable if the seller's tax position will allow the absorption of a few dollars of ordinary income.

Then again, the price might be pretty steep. Or the seller might simply refuse the terms altogether.

We're not completely at sea, however. We can use an intermediary to separate the incompatible aspects of the deal. While using an intermediary may be a bit complex, and may have its weaknesses, I have used this approach before to break such an impasse. But watch out. Without a true business purpose, a step transaction would be a sham.

What we'll need is an entity (personal or corporate) that is financially interested and willing to aid in the making of the deal for good business reasons. There are three players on the sidelines of many transactions who might qualify. They are the lawyer, the accountant, and the broker. All of these midwives to real estate deals are friendly to one side or the other. In our case, we need someone friendly to the buyer, and someone who is legally unrelated to both the buyer and the seller.

This last point is a technical one, involving what are known as the brother-sister rules of the Internal Revenue Code. These are complicated rules designed to avoid transactions between related persons. They're based on the assumption that such transactions are really not arm's length and are adverse to the interests of the Treasury.

I won't go into a long dissertation on the complexities of the brother-sister rules. An individual attempting to act as an intermediary is related to a buyer or seller if either person is related to the intermediary as a family member. Partnerships and corporate entities are deemed to be related if either the buyer or the seller holds more than 80 percent of the shares of the corporation.[1]

In most cases, a lawyer, accountant, or broker will be unrelated to the buyer and seller. Where this isn't the case, the buyer should be able to locate a friendly corporate entity in which he or she has no interest whatsoever. If an accountant is involved, for example, as a general partner of the partnership buying the property, then perhaps the lawyer or broker will be unrelated. Even if they're related, they might be doing business in a corporate format in which the clients, even if they are relatives, will have no shareholder interest.

The selection process, however, involves other considerations. Because an audit of the lawyer or the lawyer's corporation may result in breaking the attorney-client privilege, lawyers are not often selected. The attorney-client privilege is designed to preserve confidential discussions between lawyer and client, and may be particularly important in the context of tax structuring. With very few exceptions, the attorney-client privilege may be invoked to prevent the disclosure of any confidential communications between lawyer and client. Even documents may be protected under the attorney's privilege to keep his or her work product secret.

Thus, choosing the lawyer is risky. The buyer will normally want to protect the attorney-client privilege at all costs. If the privilege is broken in one respect, it is usually considered to have been broken altogether. If the IRS were successful in attacking the privilege as an inappropriate cloak to a conspiracy to defraud the government, then there would be no attorney-client privilege with respect to the transaction, and perhaps none with respect to the entire relationship. Though in some cases the risk seems worthwhile, for most people the lawyer is the last resort.

Accountants, too, are rarely chosen. Accountants are reluctant to be involved because they fear losing their independence. Far more alarming, however, is the prospect of being targeted by the IRS for frequent audits. This jeopardizes the accountant's entire livelihood. In addition, it is very likely that there is no accountant-client privilege against the disclosure of confidences. In most states, there is no such privilege and an accountant can be compelled during the course of a lawsuit to reveal the statements made by the client.

The third midwife is the broker, probably the person with the largest stake in seeing the deal fly. Regardless of whether the deal is made or not, the accountants and lawyers will still charge for their time. The broker, however, gets paid only if the transaction closes. Because of this very significant financial incentive, many brokers, if pressed, will be willing to act as the accommodating intermediary. Usually, their major concern is that they won't be paying additional taxes because of their involvement in the deal. As long as they're assured that this won't be the case, they're usually accommodating.

As an example, let's assume that the broker's wholly owned corporation is the intermediary. Even if there is some familial relationship between the broker and the buyer, the buyer will probably have no interest whatever in the broker's corporation and will be legally unrelated to it. Of course, the broker's corporation should be duly formed, adequately capitalized, and in good standing.

First, as before, there's the economic deal. This sets the purchase price and the cash requirement. The seller won't want to alter these terms. The seller wants long-term capital gain based on the purchase price and the adjusted basis. Thus, there is no opportunity to build in soft dollars by dealing directly with the seller.

Next, however, the transaction is transformed. The buyer builds in the soft dollars necessary to make the deal attractive. The cash down payment is reduced, and the differential cash is paid in ways that result in writeoffs. The purchase price is also reduced, but now the two purchase prices, of course, do not match.

Again, the reason for the involvement of the broker has

nothing to do with the tax picture. The broker has a good business reason for helping the deal along: commissions. The broker's corporation buys from the real seller and sells to the real buyer. As you'll see, the middleman will make essentially nothing more in the process than the agreed fee or commission. The rest is washed out by offsetting entries.

Suppose, for example, that we've built $100,000 in soft dollars into the deal. That means that the buyer will have $100,000 in expenses or amortizable line items while the corporate intermediary will stand to receive $100,000 in ordinary income.

In order to wash out an extra $100,000 in ordinary income that the broker's corporation doesn't really want, the intermediary must sell the property to the real buyer at a loss. Since the holding period is less than the six months required for long-term treatment, the loss is a short term loss. The intermediary buys from the seller for the seller's desired price (the one that results in long-term capital gain to the seller), but then almost immediately sells the property to the buyer for the price that was reduced in the process of building in the soft dollars. Except for the commission, of course. Whatever ordinary income is involved (other than the commission) because of the soft dollars is going to be offset by the ordinary loss. That makes the broker happy.

The result? *Everyone's* happy. The seller has a long-term capital gain based upon the desired selling price; the buyer is happy because the deal is heavily soft, thus increasing both the short-term shelter and the long-term yield; and the broker intermediary is happy because the deal has been closed and the commission earned. By the way, the broker should add a small charge to cover the cost of accounting for the two transactions.

The downside of this approach is twofold. First, it's intricate and requires professional help, which can be expensive. If the deal is large enough, however, the professional fees are well worth it. That's why we real estate lawyers are fully employed.

More important, the tax planning is open to view. Both the soft dollar deal and the economic deal have been documented for all to see *if both were seen at the same time.* The only saving grace is that the risk of audit is low and, fortunately, the IRS is not all-knowing (though it would like to believe differently). If the buyer is audited, only the soft dollar deal will be seen. It should, if the deal points are economically sound, withstand the audit. Similarly, if the seller is audited, only the normal purchase and sale can be seen. Even if the intermediary is audited, the deal is relatively safe. Lord knows, there's no law guaranteeing profits and, in parallel, no law against suffering losses.

In addition, any risk of being reversed by the IRS lies where it should—with the buyer. The seller has a perfectly normal sale to an unrelated third party, the intermediary. The soft dollars were for the buyer's benefit and the risk of losing the benefits is on the buyer's side. If there's going to be a successful attack, however, it's going to be that the structure has no economic basis.

This dance between legally unrelated parties is often the only way to break a deadlock. Since unrelated parties are free to negotiate whatever terms they like, so long as they deal in economic substance and not sham, the deal should stand up, even though it's in the open.

Actually, we perceive it as being laid bare only because we're insiders. To the rest of the world, looking from the outside in, it's still a Chinese puzzle.

NOTES

1. The gain on the sale of real property subject to depreciation between certain related persons would be ordinary income. Internal Revenue Code section 1239(b) defines "related persons" as a person and all entities that are 80 percent owned by that person. The 80 percent ownership test applies to partnership interests and shares of corporate stock held by the taxpayer and his or her spouse. Internal Revenue Code section 1239(c). For transactions between a partner and a partnership, see Internal Revenue Code section 707.

This can be a trap for the unwary. All installment sales between such related parties trigger a section in which all payments to be received in the future are deemed to have been received in the year of sale, meaning that a tax on all of it is due. Internal Revenue Code section 453(g).

See also Internal Revenue Code section 482, giving the IRS broad power to reallocate income and expense between controlled entities. If a mother rents an apartment to her daughter for a market rent, there is no problem. If the same rent is greatly below market, in order to avoid income to a high-bracket taxpayer while at the same time benefiting a loved one, the transaction could be recast. A portion of the forgiven rent could be treated as a nondeductible gift.

2. The loss is an ordinary loss, as opposed to a capital loss, because the property was acquired for resale in connection with earning a commission and not for investment or business purposes.

17

Structuring Business Buyouts

For our second master class, let's take another example, but this time from a different arena. Instead of a real estate deal, let's try our cookbook on a business deal.

This case study is also taken from an actual situation. My client was referred by a certified public accountant for documentation purposes. The deal had already been signed. Because of that, I was barely able to catch the deal in time, and only because the sellers were still willing to negotiate. In the usual case, I would have gotten there too late.

I found the seller's willingness to negotiate a bit irregular. When the contract is signed, the negotiation is usually over. When they hired me after the deal was signed, my clients were either asking for little more than a classroom lecture on their rights and obligations, or they were seeking my services as a scrivener (a mere draftsman) to properly document their deal.

I took the willingness to negotiate after the contract had been signed as an indication of weakness and desperation on the seller's part. I was right.

My clients were buying a specialty store in a prominent hotel in downtown Los Angeles. There was inventory, leasehold improvements, the potential of competition from our seller, and equipment. The *stuff* of tax planning, hidden like those proverbial diamonds in the rough.

As signed, the contract contained no allocations and no consulting agreements or convenants of any kind. There was no tax planning at all. The buyers were to pay a purchase price of $60,000 with inventory estimated at $15,000. The price was to be paid with $20,000 cash and a $40,000 promissory note with a security interest in the furniture, fixtures, and leasehold equipment. If the inventory was less, then the price, and note, would be reduced accordingly.

Before I go on, note that the effects of good tax planning are evident even in a smallish deal. The soft dollar technique works regardless of the amount of money involved. The goal is a better return on whatever amount of money is involved in the deal. The usefulness of the technique is directly applicable to *any* deal, regardless of size.

In this case, the world was open to me. While such freedom is often confusing, my cookbook indicated that certain ingredients could be employed. I began to stir up a recipe.

There are two ways to buy a business. If the business has a corporate format, you can buy the stock and, with it, both the assets and the liabilities. Stock is an intangible and lumps assets and liabilities together. After the lumping, there should be something left over. In the familiar parlance of finance, assets minus liabilities equals net worth, or shareholder equity. That equity is the net "book value" of the stock. It's the corporate equivalent of iceberg equity. It's recovered only when the stock is sold to someone else—for a profit, one hopes.

As an individual buyer, there are times when you might want to buy stock. I've done it before for my own portfolio. Generally, though, there's no tax advantage to it. Even if you use a new section (section 388, passed in 1984) to allocate the purchase price to the assets, and thereby achieve an increased basis, you'll have to form an "acquiring corporation" and realize that the tax planning benefits wil remain at the corporate level.[1] The only tax advantage to owning stock usually is the capital gain treatment when you sell. Then any gain over the basis of the stock will be capital gain, assuming the requisite holding period.

The other way to buy a business is to buy its assets. We can buy assets like inventory, equipment, accounts receivable, leasehold improvements, and real estate. Since it's the assets of a business that go to work earning income, buying all, or substantially all, of the assets is the equivalent of buying the entire business. Such asset transactions are grist for a tax planner's mill. After we've struck our economic deal, which always comes first, we can allocate some small portion of the purchase price to control the name, trademarks, and service marks of the business. These are the specific representations of "goodwill."

Then we'll go on to allocate the lion's share of the purchase price to those hard-working assets like equipment and real estate, taking care to keep the allocations within the bounds of economic reality—perhaps at the level of what it might cost to buy these assets on the open market at retail.

There are some sources of conflict, however. Goodwill is usually the source of some debate between buyer and seller. Sellers in an asset transaction want their premium, if any, associated with goodwill. Because goodwill is an asset, the premium would be capital gain and taxed accordingly. But buyers don't like to pay for goodwill because goodwill can't be written off. In an asset transaction, goodwill is equivalent to shareholder's equity. It's a deadwood, nonworking asset.

The other road to conflict involves short-term agreements restricting competition, usually called "covenants-not-to-compete." These covenants, because they're short-term, can be amortized over one or two years. That's good for the buyer, but anathema for many sellers. They must treat the income associated with the covenant as ordinary income, not capital gain.

So, buyers want covenants, consulting agreements, and the like; sellers don't. Sellers want any premium over book value associated with goodwill; buyers don't.

Before I return to my example, let me make a comment. These are two major areas of conflict, but to tell the truth, the conflict can often be one of principle. A business worth $60,000 can't have much in the way of goodwill. Nor can the threat of competition from the seller be very great. Overdoing the negotiation in these areas could kill the deal.

Now let's go back to our case study. As you may recall, my client's purchase price was $60,000, including inventory. If the inventory was found to be less than $15,000, the purchase price and note were to be adjusted.

Naturally, what I needed to do was to create a number of asset categories and make allocations to them, realizing that some categories would carry additional benefits like ITCs. In

Figure 17-1, you'll see how I modified the deal. In Appendix F, I've included the addendum that was attached to the original printed form purchase agreement and deposit receipt that had been supplied by the broker (I've changed the addendum slightly to protect the identity of my client). The additional terms were incorporated by reference and, to the extent of any conflict with the deposit receipt, designated as being controlling.

1.	Furniture & fixtures	$ 3,500.00
2.	Equipment	12,500.00
3.	Leasehold improvements	15,000.00
4.	Covenant-not-to-compete	12,000.00
5.	License (beer & wine)	1,000.00
6.	Trade name	1,000.00
7.	Inventory	15,000.00
	Total	$60,000.00

Figure 17-1. Allocations of Purchase Price.

By the way, you should note that the broker wasn't interested in any tax planning. The broker was interested in a signature and a commission.

As you can see, the allocations were to the kinds of ingredients we've been discussing throughout the book. The covenant was for six months and covered a three-mile radius. Thus, it was a first year writeoff. I was able to induce a large covenant relative to goodwill and the beer and wine license because the seller was indifferent to the tax consequences. He simply needed the deal and the cash.

The furniture, fixtures, and equipment could be depreciated over the usual five years and, of course, qualified for an ITC for used property. The leasehold improvements could be written off over the life of the lease, which, for illustration purposes, I'll say was fifteen years.

What have we done? Before using the soft dollar approach, my clients were going to pay $20,000 cash for the business. Without an allocation, it would have been difficult to write any of it off. In Figure 17-2, you can see the results: Most of the

$20,000 cash paid in was written off during the first two years of ownership.

	1st Year	2nd Year	3rd Year	Three-Year Totals
Amortization				
Covenant	$12,000	—	—	$12,000
Depreciation				
Furniture, Fixtures, & Equipment ($16,000 ÷ 5)	3,200	3,200	3,200	9,600
Leasehold Improvements ($15,000 ÷ 15)	1,000	1,000	1,000	3,000
ITCs				
Furniture, Fixtures, & Equipment (used; 6%)	960	—	—	960
Totals	$17,160	4,200	4,200	$25,560

Figure 17-2.   Effect of Allocations.

The deal was vastly better and my clients thanked me after they saw the effect on the next tax return. As you can see from Figure 17-2, the writeoffs for the first two years amounted to roughly $21,360 (ignoring the different effect of the ITC as a credit). Of the $45,000 in assets other than inventory, over one-third was expensed in the first year and almost one-half by the end of the second year. And by the end of the second year, *all* of the cash paid over had been written off. If my clients were in the 30 percent tax bracket, the soft dollar technique was good for $7,668 ($25,560 × 30 percent), reducing their real equity from $20,000 to $12,332. Had they sold for a $15,000 profit after the first three years, the yield would have been 121.6 percent ($15,000 ÷ $12,332) and they would have more than doubled their money. The annual average yield would have been roughly forty percent. Without the soft dollar technique, the same $15,000 profit would have returned only 75 percent over three years, or an average annual yield of only 25 percent. The soft dollar technique was, therefore, responsible for improving the situation (assuming a $15,000 profit on day one of year four (to avoid any recapture of the ITC)) by just about 50 percent. A 25 percent average annual yield was turned into a forty percent return just because we worked smart at the time of acquisition.

The important point to remember is that, while some allocation can properly be made in any such deal, the opportunity to control the situation comes during the initial negotiations, not after. By using the soft dollar technique when you can, you can do something that every tax planner endeavors to do: By using your knowledge of the law, you can negotiate terms that, when properly expressed, will take advantage of all the deductibility involved.

NOTES

1. Under a provision added in 1984, an acquiring corporation may buy the stock of a target and, in the agreement, allocate the purchase price to various assets. This enables the acquiring corporation to step up the basis of the assets being acquired, which in turn means that there will be greater depreciation writeoffs. Internal Revenue Code section 388. For individuals acquiring stock, however, there's no authority for such allocations. You'd have to form a corporation and use section 388, or buy assets as in the example in the text.

18

Sham Dollars

From what has been said in earlier chapters, it should be clear now that there are a number of things to avoid. A short checklist of things to avoid should come quickly to mind: a down payment, to the extent it represents iceberg equity, and the purchase of stock or an allocation to goodwill when buying a business. While you can recover from these goods at a later date—when you sell, any increase will be long-term capital gain—the opportunity for a tax-structured "buy" will have been missed.

By far the most common mistake is the failure to make allocations, whether buying real estate or the assets of a company. Simply by making reasonable allocations to balance sheet items that generate depreciation deductions or, better still, both depreciation deductions and investment tax credits, you simultaneously achieve two things: (1) more writeoffs and (2) a better yield for the money that's tied up in the deal.

The checklist of things to look for should come just as readily to mind: structures; furniture, fixtures, and equipment; leasehold improvements; agreements and covenants; and seller financing using all-inclusive notes. As I've said, allocations to structures and FF&E are sometimes free for the asking. The seller may face recapture on the structure, and will face recapture on the FF&E, but that will be true in every case. Selling triggers it. The seller can achieve a long-term capital gain from their sale regardless of whether they're sold in bulk or sold separately. While allocations to contracts and convenants may result in ordinary income to the seller for services rendered, there are many who won't mind this at all: dealers, sellers willing to absorb some ordinary income, and sellers needing cash so desperately that they choose to ignore the adverse tax consequences.

Once you see that there's a pot with which to cook, the recipes are easy. Your goal should be to maximize your return on the working equity. The soft dollar technique, used properly, is a powerful and legal way to reduce the number of dollars tied up in a deal and to increase your return.

The soft dollar structuring that I've illustrated in this book is also designed to help deals happen. It is designed to sweeten the deal for the buyer without hurting the seller. A smart seller will even *offer* soft dollars to a buyer as a closing technique. Once these techniques are part of your negotiating vocabulary, you'll be working with intentions that are tax-smart. From there, it's simply a matter of working out the details in the negotiations and clearly writing them into the agreements.

In some cases, a hybrid situation will come up. I can recall one situation in which the sellers wanted to retire. They were going to sell their business, but wanted to sell it lock, stock, and barrel. That meant that the buyer had to buy stock, which precluded much tax planning. Fortunately, they also wanted to sell the office building they owned (their business was the largest tenant) and that allowed for an allocation of the total price primarily to the real estate. While there wasn't very much room for maneuvering, the situation did highlight the value of a good price as distinguished from tax-structured terms. The tax structuring is the icing; it is not the cake. The bottom line is a property or business that is well bought. Well bought is half sold. If you jeopardize a good deal by pushing too hard for a better tax structure, you'll be throwing the baby out with the bathwater.

Let me show you the danger of stretching the point too far. In its complaint against International Systems and Controls Corporation (ISC) and its officers, the Securities and Exchange Commission (SEC) alleged that the chairman and chief executive had misappropriated $160,000 of the corporation's funds to buy a large house and an eighty-five-acre farm outside of Dublin, Ireland. The chief executive took title in his own name, but for eight years, from 1970 to 1978, the company paid over $1 million to purchase, decorate, and maintain the property.

ISC described this property, in its public reports (including its 1978 report to the SEC), as "approximately 15,000 square feet of office space, support facilities, and visitor accommodations." The only office space, however, was the den, the library, and a desk, typewriter, and telex in the basement, which were used when the chief executive's personal secretary accompanied him to the house.

The expenses were concealed by using a London subsidiary of the company, something called ISCEurope. ISCEurope paid the bills, added 3 percent, and recorded the total as a receivable from the parent company. The parent repaid the subsidiary and called the payments "consultancy" fees, which were, in turn, charged to selling, engineering, and administrative accounts of the parent.

Needless to say, this didn't work. The point of the story is twofold. One lesson is that people seem highly motivated to evade the law. It's likely that many people have tried, some successfully, to hide from the IRS.

In the case of the ISC, for example, the retirement home for the chief executive could have been booked as compensation to him and an expense to the corporation. But then he'd have had to pay income tax on the money. Assuming that the money spent for the purchase, furnishing, and maintenance of the farm would have been paid to him as compensation, and assuming that he was in the 50 percent (then it was 70 percent) tax bracket, the whole venture would have been twice as expensive. As it turned out, the expense and embarrassment of being caught were discounted too much.

The second lesson is that calling something a "consultancy fee" is by no means a sufficient reason for believing that the disbursement is an expense. There must be a real understanding that the seller can provide some continuing help to the buyer, even if paid in advance. In the ISC case, the label was a complete deception. The agreement must obligate the seller to provide services, even if the buyer never calls upon the seller to do so. Finally, the agreement must bear some reasonable relationship to the marketplace and the deal. Without some rational basis (bids from others or some evidence of comparative costs), the fees will be attacked as a mere sham. The difference between sham and substance[1] is the same as that between planning your affairs wisely to minimize taxes and the criminal act of tax evasion.

You might also surmise, after reading about ISC's predicament, that the SEC and the IRS have seen such shams before. They have. While I believe in being aggressive about the tax laws, care must be used to avoid stepping beyond the bounds of sound business practice. Each document in a deal must have real economic substance, and proper documentation must be in the file. The cost of research and preparation must be viewed as a necessary transaction cost and the equivalent of insurance, especially since such "consultancy fees" may be a red flag for an enterprising investigator to audit the entire deal. You might be interested in making money; others are interested in making a name for themselves by catching you in foul territory.

NOTES

1. For a discussion of the "sham transaction doctrine," *see Estate of Martin Melche, et al.* v. *Comm.,* 29 TC Memo 1010 (1970).

19

Tax Avoidance Philosophy

This book has been an excursion through the difficult terrain of our tax laws. Some will say that I've taken advantage of loopholes. Some will say that I've seen loopholes where there are none. One of my major goals was to explain, in simple terms, how sophisticated professionals use the law to put their deals together.

In the end, the sophisticated structuring of deals boils down to philosophy and interpretation. The study of law, including tax law (dense though it may be), is the study of language. In every word, sentence, and paragraph of every law and every contract there are the plain, ordinary meanings of words used in everyday conversation. Words can, however, take on specialized meanings, and many of them have secondary meanings. In every contract, for example, there are sentences written for the benefit of the buyer, on the one hand, and the seller, on the other. It's hard to write a completely neutral document, which is the reason that ambiguities are often construed against the person preparing the text.

Before studying the nuances of the tax laws, however, a working knowledge of the rules in their basic operation is absolutely essential. What I've done in this book is to present some rather basic rules and use them in the way common language would have them used in different business contexts. In some cases, I'm well within the rules. At other times, while I'm not on the frontier of interpretation, the issue, on audit, could go against the taxpayer if the agent doesn't understand the transaction or if the particular facts don't support the position being taken.

In this book I have tried, first, to present the rules themselves in an environment where you can see them in operation. Second, I've tried to let you see how, with further study, you can become familiar with the rules and use them to accurately describe your transaction. I have tried to open your mind so that you can ask better and more challenging questions of the legal and accounting professionals who advise you.

In one respect, these professionals debate the issues I've been raising every time they design a deal. The conservative approach, of course, is to stay within the core meaning of the Internal Revenue Code and the regulations and cases interpreting it. This approach is designed to avoid an audit altogether.

Even more important, the documentation available for review must be the reflection of the true intent of the parties. As I said, the art involved in a good design is the appearance of no design at all. It is vital to put the lessons of this book to use on day one of the negotiations. You should *never* document a deal one way, then change it later in order to build in soft dollars. You should *never* backdate the paperwork to make it appear as if these considerations were always a part of the discussions. Such conduct, because it's strictly for tax reasons, not economic reasons, is evasion and fraud.

Why take the risk? When a deal accurately reflects the true intentions of the parties and is properly documented, I don't think it's likely for even the most sophisticated IRS agent to put together a strong case for reversing the deal, and I say that knowing that the burden of proof is on the taxpayer. If the deal structure is rational and the documentation well done, the agent is going to have to figure out what your thinking was. Powerful though they may be, they're not mind readers.

The only alternative for the IRS is to compare the deal structure with the marketplace, in hopes of showing it to be unreasonable, and therefore a sham. The built-in safeguard against this, however, is that we designed the terms so that they would have a reasonable relationship to the marketplace in the first place. In addition, the effort required to show the deal up, by comparing it to the marketplace, involves a great deal of work. Unless you've become a target, the IRS has more cost-effective things to do with its time.

With our cookbook of tax-smart ingredients, we can better handle all of those worthwhile deals that require some cash. The deals requiring no cash are usually deals involving either a poor piece of property or too much debt. From my experience, cash is required 99 percent of the time in deals worth making. With the soft-dollar technique at your command, however, you'll be able to negotiate deals that are close to being "nothing down." While others may claim that they buy real estate with "nothing down," remember this book. There is a better way.

Appendix A
Depreciation Schedules

TABLE 1. 150 PERCENT DECLINING-BALANCE METHOD: PERSONAL PROPERTY

Table 1 incorporates the 150 percent declining-balance method of depreciation. It converts to the straight-line method at the optimum time. It is for personal property placed in service after December 31, 1980, and before January 1, 1985. The figures are in percents for each class of property.

Recovery Year	3-Year	5-Year	10-Year	15-Year Public Utility
1	25	15	8	5
2	38	22	14	10
3	37	21	12	9
4		21	10	8
5		21	10	7
6			10	7
7			9	6
8			9	6
9			9	6
10			9	6
11				6
12				6
13				6
14				6
15				6
Total	100	100	100	100

Table 1. Personal property percentages for 1981–1984.

TABLE 2. 175 PERCENT DECLINING-BALANCE METHOD: PERSONAL PROPERTY

Table 2 incorporates the 175 percent declining-balance method of depreciation. It converts to the straight-line method at the optimum time. It is for personal property placed in service after January 1, 1985, and before December 31, 1985. The figures are in percents for each class of property.

Recovery Year	3-Year	5-Year	10-Year	15-Year Public Utility
1	29	18	9	6
2	47	33	19	12
3	24	25	16	12
4		16	14	11
5		8	12	10
6			10	9
7			8	8
8			6	7
9			4	6
10			2	5
11				4
12				4
13				3
14				2
15				1
Total	100	100	100	100

Table 2. Personal property percentages for 1985.

TABLE 3. 200 PERCENT DECLINING-BALANCE METHOD: PERSONAL PROPERTY

Table 3 incorporates the 200 percent declining-balance method of depreciation. It converts to the straight-line method at the optimum time. It is for personal property placed in service at any time after December 31, 1985. The figures are in percents for each class of property.

Recovery Year	3-Year	5-Year	10-Year	15-Year Public Utility
1	33	20	10	7
2	45	32	18	12
3	22	24	16	12
4		16	14	11
5		8	12	10
6			10	9
7			8	8
8			6	7
9			4	6
10			2	5
11				4
12				3
13				3
14				2
15				1
Total	100	100	100	100

Table 3. Personal property percentages for 1986 and thereafter.

TABLE 4. 175 PERCENT DECLINING BALANCE METHOD: REAL PROPERTY

Percentages for eighteen-year real property acquired after June 22, 1984, using accelerated depreciation
(Assuming Mid-Month Convention)

If the Recovery Year is:	And the Month in the First Recovery Year the Property is Placed in Service is:											
	1	2	3	4	5	6	7	8	9	10	11	12
	The applicable percentage is:											
1	9	9	8	7	6	5	4	4	3	2	1	0.4
2	9	9	9	9	9	9	9	9	9	10	10	10.0
3	8	8	8	8	8	8	8	8	9	9	9	9.0
4	7	7	7	7	7	8	8	8	8	8	8	8.0
5	7	7	7	7	7	7	7	7	7	7	7	7.0
6	6	6	6	6	6	6	6	6	6	6	6	6.0
7	5	5	5	5	6	6	6	6	6	6	6	6.0
8	5	5	5	5	5	5	5	5	5	5	5	5.0
9	5	5	5	5	5	5	5	5	5	5	5	5.0
10	5	5	5	5	5	5	5	5	5	5	5	5.0
11	5	5	5	5	5	5	5	5	5	5	5	5.0
12	5	5	5	5	5	5	5	5	5	5	5	5.0
13	4	4	4	5	4	4	5	4	4	4	5	5.0
14	4	4	4	4	4	4	4	4	4	4	4	4.0
15	4	4	4	4	4	4	4	4	4	4	4	4.0
16	4	4	4	4	4	4	4	4	4	4	4	4.0
17	4	4	4	4	4	4	4	4	4	4	4	4.0
18	4	3	4	4	4	4	4	4	4	4	4	4.0
19		1	1	1	2	2	2	3	3	3	3	3.6

Sample use of table: If a calendar year domestic taxpayer places eighteen-year real property in service in August 1985, the cost recovery schedule indicates, using column 8, that 4 percent would apply in the first year, 9 percent in the second year, and so on. If the property had an unadjusted basis of $100,000, the 1985 allowance would be $4,000 ($100,000 × .04), the 1986 allowance would be $9,000 ($100,000 × .09), and so on. The table above automatically switches from 175 percent declining balance to straight line at a time that maximizes the amounts deductible. It is taken directly from a table published by the United States Treasury Department.

TABLE 5. STRAIGHT LINE METHOD: REAL PROPERTY

Percentages for eighteen-year real property acquired after June 22, 1984, using straight-line method
(Assuming Mid-Month Convention)

If the Recovery Year is:	And the Month in the First Recovery Year the Property is Placed in Service is:					
	1-2	3-4	5-7	8-9	10-11	12
	The applicable percentage is:					
1	5	4	3	2	1	0.2
2	6	6	6	6	6	6.0
3	6	6	6	6	6	6.0
4	6	6	6	6	6	6.0
5	6	6	6	6	6	6.0
6	6	6	6	6	6	6.0
7	6	6	6	6	6	6.0
8	6	6	6	6	6	6.0
9	6	6	6	6	6	6.0
10	6	6	6	6	6	6.0
11	5	5	5	5	5	5.8
12	5	5	5	5	5	5.0
13	5	5	5	5	5	5.0
14	5	5	5	5	5	5.0
15	5	5	5	5	5	5.0
16	5	5	5	5	5	5.0
17	5	5	5	5	5	5.0
18	5	5	5	5	5	5.0
19	1	2	3	4	5	5.0

Sample use of table: This table is used in exactly the same way as the 175 percent declining balance table. This is the eighteen-year straight-line method using a mid-month convention.

Appendix B
Sample Consulting Agreement

CONSULTING AGREEMENT

Caution: Use of this agreement, because of the percentage compensation clause in paragraph 4, may require a real estate brokerage license.

THIS AGREEMENT, entered into this ___ day of _____, at _____, _____, by and between _____ (hereinafter referred to as "Consultant"), and _____ (hereinafter referred to as "Principal").

RECITALS

It is the desire of Principal to develop certain real property ("the Property") formerly owned by Consultant (which real property is legally described in Exhibit "A" attached hereto and incorporated herein by this reference) and, in so doing, to gain the benefit of Consultant's past experience in connection with the Property, including, but not limited to, Consultant's past dealings with architects, engineers, and local and state governmental agencies, and further, to gain Consultant's assistance in obtaining industrial development bond financing ("Financing") for improvements to the Property.

It is the desire of Consultant to introduce to Principal architects, engineers, and representatives of local and state governmental agencies who have knowledge of the Property and any person or any governmental agency capable of arranging or providing Financing for improvements to the Property in exchange for the remuneration provided for herein.

144

NOW, THEREFORE, it is agreed by the parties hereto as follows:

1. *Term.* The respective duties and obligations of the parties hereto shall commence on the date hereof and shall terminate on _____, a period of one (1) year.

2. *Consultations.* Consultant shall be available for consultation with Principal at reasonable times concerning matters pertaining to the subject matter hereof.

3. *Reports.* Consultant shall render such oral or written reports as may from time to time be reasonably necessary to accomplish the purposes hereunder.

4. *Compensation.* In addition to other compensation provided for herein, Consultant shall receive from Principal a flat fee in the amount of _____ dollars ($_____) for the performance of the services to be rendered to Principal pursuant to the terms of this Agreement. Said fee is due and payable upon the Closing of an escrow for the purchase of the Property by Principal and sale by Consultant, as per the terms and conditions of that certain Agreement between the parties dated _____. Consultant shall also receive one percent (1%) of the net proceeds provided to Principal as a result of any Financing arranged by Consultant. Other than as specified hereinabove, Consultant hereby waives and relinquishes any rights Consultant might otherwise have to any and all expense reimbursements, finder's fees, broker's commissions, or any other similar payment arising upon the performance of said services.

5. *Minimum Amount of Service.* Consultant shall devote such time to the affairs of Principal as the Principal, in its sole discretion, may require in connection with all services other than the arranging or obtaining of Financing for the Property. With respect to arranging or obtaining such Financing, Consultant shall devote only such time as may be required for their best efforts.

6. *Limited Liability.* With regard to the services to be performed by Consultant pursuant to the terms of this Agreement, Consultant shall not be liable to Principal, or to anyone who may claim any right due to his relationship with Principal, for any acts or omissions in the performance of said services on the part of Consultant or on the part of the agents or employees of

Consultant; except when said acts or omissions of Consultant are due to their willful and malicious misconduct. Principal holds Consultant free and harmless from any obligations, costs, claims, judgments, and attorneys' fees arising from or growing out of the services rendered to Principal pursuant to the terms of this Agreement or in any way connected with the rendering of said services, except when the same shall arise due to the willful and malicious misconduct of Consultant.

7. *Attorneys' Fees.* If any action at law or in equity is necessary to enforce or interpret the terms of this Agreement, the prevailing party shall be entitled to reasonable attorneys' fees.

8. *Governing Law.* This Agreement shall be binding on and shall be for the benefit of the parties hereto and their respective heirs, executors, administrators, successors, and assigns, and shall be governed by the laws of the State of _____.

9. *Headings.* The headings contained herein are for convenience only and are not to be given weight in construing this Agreement.

10. *Assignment.* This Agreement may not be assigned by any party hereto, nor may the duties of any party be assigned or assumed by a third party.

EXECUTED at _____, _____, on the day and year first above written.

Principal:

Dated: _____   By _____

Consultant

Dated: _____   By _____

Appendix C

Sample Rent-Guarantee Agreement

RENT UP AND GUARANTEE AGREEMENT

In order to guarantee a minimum monthly rental level from that certain residential income property located at _____, _____ (hereinafter the "Property"), _____ (hereinafter "Seller"), in consideration of the receipt of _____ dollars ($_____) from _____ (hereinafter "Buyer") does hereby warrant, covenant, and guarantee:

That Buyer shall have a monthly offset against payments made under a promissory note executed in favor of Seller in an amount equal to the difference between the actual monthly rentals collected from the Property during each of the ___ ( ) months following the close of escrow and the sum of _____ ($_____) per month. The offset in said amount shall constitute a direct reduction from each note installment due during the period prescribed.

Executed this ___ day of _____ at _____.

SELLER:

Dated: _____   By _____

BUYER

Dated: _____   By _____

Appendix D

Sample Covenant-Not-to-Compete

COVENANT-NOT-TO-COMPETE

THIS COVENANT-NOT-TO-COMPETE is effective this ___ day of _____, by and between _____ ("Covenantor" hereinafter) and _____ ("Covenantee" hereinafter).

WHEREAS, Covenantor is in the business of developing, owning, leasing, selling, managing, and operating residential apartment buildings;

WHEREAS, Covenantor is and has been in the business of developing, owning, leasing, managing, and operating the property located at _____, _____, _____, legally described on Exhibit A attached hereto and incorporated herein by this reference (the "Property" hereinafter), and in developing, owning, leasing, managing, and operating other residential properties throughout the County of _____, State of _____;

WHEREAS, Covenantor is selling the Property to Covenantee so that Covenantee may undertake Covenantor's business of owning, leasing, managing, and operating the Property; and

WHEREAS, this Convenant-Not-to-Compete is given to Covenantee in connection with the purchase by Covenantee of all of Covenantor's goodwill in its business of developing, owning, leasing, managing, and operating the Property, and to benefit Covenantee by relieving Covenantee from the prospective competitive activities of Covenantor in connection with said Property in order to maximize the likelihood that said Property will be operated in the most successful manner and will be able to be rented without competing in the residential rental market with similar new apartment buildings owned, operated, or developed by Covenantor;

NOW, THEREFORE, it is agreed by the parties hereto that Covenantor covenants not to compete with Covenantee, in the manner hereinafter described, for the consideration set forth below.

1. *Covenant.* Covenantor shall not engage, directly or indirectly, in the business of developing and constructing a residential apartment building and thereafter leasing, managing, or operating such newly constructed residential apartment building for a period commencing the date hereof through _____, at any location within a radius of one (1) mile of the Property. Covenantor furthermore represents and agrees that he will not, directly or indirectly, solicit or otherwise induce any of the existing tenants of the Property (a) to vacate their tenancy of the Property, or (b) to locate their residence in any location within a radius of one (1) mile of the Property, or in any residential property in which Covenantor may have an interest in the future during the term of this convenant.

Notwithstanding the foregoing, Covenantor may manage, operate, and lease the Property as a principal, partner, or employee of any person or entity selected by Covenantee to manage the Property.

For purposes of this section, Covenantor includes any persons or entities that are directly or indirectly controlled by Covenantor or of which Covenantor is a shareholder, partner, officer, director, trustee, or employee.

2. *Consideration for Covenant.* Covenantee agrees to pay Covenantor, as consideration for the foregoing covenant, the sum of _____ dollars ($_____).

3. *Terms of Payment.* Payment of the consideration for this Covenant-Not-to-Compete shall be payable on or before _____, _____ (date).

4. *Default by Covenantor.* In the event of a default hereunder, Covenantee shall be entitled to seek injunctive relief, as well as other legal remedies to which he may be entitled. Covenantor acknowledges that, in the event of a breach by Covenantor

hereunder, Covenantee does not have an adequate remedy at law.

5. *Attorneys' Fees*. In the event legal action is brought to enforce the obligations of either of the parties hereto, the prevailing party in such action shall be entitled to receive reasonable attorneys' fees and costs incurred in the prosecution of such suit as a part of any award by any court of competent jurisdiction.

6. *Governing Law*. In the event of suit hereunder, the parties agree that the courts of the State of _____ shall have personal jurisdiction over them and this covenant shall be construed under the laws of the State of _____.

7. *Adequacy of Consideration*. It is acknowledged that Covenantee has purchased the Property from Covenantor. The Property is newly constructed and Covenantee is the first user of the Property. By virtue thereof, the profitable operation of the Property depends upon the ability of Covenantee to fully rent the Property at projected rental levels. Should Covenantor complete a new apartment project for rental within six (6) months of Covenantee's acquisition of the Property, Covenantee would be seriously impaired in his ability to attain the desired rental levels for the Property. It is further acknowledged that were Covenantor to complete a new residential apartment building for occupancy, within six (6) months, Covenantor would, by conservative estimates, be able to derive, through immediate resale upon completion of construction of such a property, an amount at least equal to _____ dollars ($_____). In recognition of the foregoing facts, it is agreed that the consideration is adequate for the covenant herein granted.

8. *Headings*. Headings are for convenience only and shall not be used in construing any section hereof.

9. *Miscellaneous*. This Convenant-Not-to-Compete contains the entire agreement between the parties with respect to the subject matter hereof and may be amended solely by an instrument in writing executed by both parties.

IN WITNESS WHEREOF, the parties hereto affix their signatures at _____, _____ on the date first hereinabove stated.

COVENANTOR:

Dated: _____   By _____

COVENANTEE:

Dated: _____   By _____

Appendix E

Sample Property-Management Agreement

PROFESSIONAL MANAGEMENT AGREEMENT

In consideration of the covenants herein contained, _____ (hereinafter called "Owner"), and _____ (hereinafter called "Agent"), agree as follows:

1. Owner hereby employs Agent exclusively to rent, lease, operate, and manage the property known as _____, in _____ (hereinafter called the "Premises"), upon the terms hereinafter set forth, beginning on the date of acquisition of the Premises by Owner and terminating on _____, which is the final and complete termination date of this contract.

2. Agent accepts the employment and agrees:

(a) To use diligence in the management of the Premises for the period and upon the terms herein provided, and to furnish the services of his/her organization for the renting, leasing, operating, and managing of the Premises.

(b) To render monthly statements of receipts, expenses, and charges and to remit to Owner, or retain in an account for Owner's benefit to be used for disbursements for the benefit of Owner, receipts less disbursements. In the event the disbursements shall be in excess of the rents collected by Agent, Owner hereby agrees to pay such excess promptly upon demand of Agent.

(c) To deposit all receipts collected for Owner (less any sums properly deducted or otherwise provided herein) in a Trust account in a national or state institution qualified to engage in the banking or trust business, separate from Agent's personal account. All checks drawn on such account shall require the signature of _____. However, Agent will not be held liable in event of bankruptcy or failure of a depository.

(d) That Agent's employees who handle or are responsible for Owner's monies shall be bonded by a fidelity bond in an adequate amount.

3. Owner hereby gives to Agent the following authority and powers and agrees to assume the expenses in connection herewith:

(a) To advertise the availability for rental of the Premises or any part thereof, and to display "for rent" signs thereon; to sign, renew and/or cancel leases for the Premises or any part thereof; to collect rents or other charges and expenses due or to become due and give receipts therefor; to terminate tenancies and to sign and serve in the name of Owner such notices as are appropriate; to institute and prosecute actions; to evict tenants and to recover possession of the Premises; to sue for and in the name of Owner and recover rents and other sums due; and when expedient, to settle, compromise, and release such actions or suits or reinstate such tenancies. Any lease executed for Owner by Agent shall not exceed six (6) months without approval of Owner.

(b) To make or cause to be made and supervise repairs and alterations, and to do decorating on the Premises; to purchase supplies and pay all bills therefor.

(c) To hire, discharge, and supervise all labor and employees required for the operation and maintenance of the Premises; it being agreed that all employees shall be deemed employees of Owner and not Agent, and that Agent may perform any of its duties through Owner's attorneys, agents, or employees and shall not be responsible for their acts, defaults, or negligence if reasonable care has been exercised in their appointment and retention.

(d) To make contracts for electricity, gas, fuel, water, telephone, window cleaning, ash or rubbish hauling, and other services or such of them as Agent shall deem advisable; Owner to assume the obligation of any contract so entered into at the termination of this agreement.

(e) To pay mortgage indebtedness, property and employee taxes, and special assessments and to place necessary insurance.

4. Owner further agrees:

(a) To indemnify and save Agent completely harmless from any and all costs, expenses, attorneys' fees, suits, liabilities, damages, or claim for damages, including but not limited to those arising out of any injury or death to any person or persons or damage to any property of any kind whatsoever and to whomsoever belonging, including Owner, in any way relating to the management of the Premises by Agent or the performance or exercise of any of the duties, obligations, powers, or authorities herein or hereafter granted to Agent; to carry, at Owner's sole cost and expense, such public liability, property damage, and worker's compensation insurance as shall be adequate to protect the interests of Agent and Owner, the policies that shall name Agent as well as Owner as the party insured. Agent shall not be liable for any error of judgment or for any mistake of fact or law, or for anything that it may do or refrain from doing, except in cases of willful misconduct or gross negligence.

(b) To pay Agent five percent (5%) of all gross receipts derived from the operation of the Property payable ten (10) days after the end of each month. Such fee shall be paid as follows: _____.

5. This agreement shall be binding upon the successors and assigns of Agent, and the heirs, administrators, executors, successors, and assigns of Owner.

6. Owner shall have the right to terminate this agreement on thirty (30) days' written notice to Agent.

7. If it shall become necessary for Agent or Owner to give notice of any kind, the same shall be given, and shall be complete, by sending such notice by registered mail to the address shown under the signature below.

IN WITNESS WHEREOF, the parties hereto have affixed or caused to be affixed their respective signatures this ___ day of _____, 19___.

CONSULTANT:

Dated: _____   By _____

PRINCIPAL:

Dated: _____   By _____

Appendix F

Addendum to Purchase Agreement and Deposit Receipt

**ADDENDUM
TO PURCHASE AGREEMENT AND DEPOSIT
RECEIPT**

1. *Terms:*

Cash through escrow	$20,000
Promissory Note with security interest in furniture, fixtures, and leasehold improvements	40,000
Total	$60,000

The Promissory Note given shall be payable $849.89 or more per month, including ten percent (10%) interest per annum all due in sixty (60) months. In the event the landlord increases the rent from six percent (6%) of gross receipts and instead demands the stated guaranteed minimum rental in the existing lease, the unpaid principal shall be due at the end of the seventy-second (72nd) month.

2. *Allocation of Purchase Price:*

The purchase price will be allocated according to the following schedule:

Furniture & Fixtures	$ 3,500
Leasehold Improvements	15,000
Equipment	12,500
License (Beer & Wine)	1,000
Trade Name (goodwill)	1,000
Inventory	15,000
Covenant-Not-to-Compete	12,000
Total	$60,000

3. *Name and Vesting:*

The purchaser herein is _____, a California corporation, hereinafter referred to as Buyer.

4. *Assignment of Name:*

Seller hereby transfers, sells, and assigns to Buyer all right, title, and interest in the name "_____." Seller agrees to change its corporate name or dissolve immediately after this transaction is consummated. In the event Seller fails to do so, Seller covenants and agrees, for itself and its successors, that it shall not do business of any kind with the general public in its corporate name and must choose a fictitious business name if it does so. Seller acknowledges that Buyer's remedy at law would be inadequate if Seller breaches this agreement and that Buyer may seek and have all remedies afforded by a court of equity, including injunctive relief.

5. *Restrictive Covenant-Not-to-Compete:*

Seller agrees to execute the Covenant-Not-to-Compete that is attached hereto and incorporated herein. Said covenant shall survive the close of escrow. [Note: the form of covenant used in this transaction is not included in this Appendix, but is included in the book as Appendix B.]

6. *Temporary Permit and Early Possession:*

Buyer shall take possession of the premises on _____, and all prorations shall be made as of that date. Buyer shall be responsible for all current liabilities incurred after _____. Seller shall cooperate with Buyer so that Buyer may obtain a temporary beer and wine retail permit. During the time prior to transfer of Seller's license to Buyer, Seller shall execute any documents necessary for Buyer to be granted said permit. The fees and costs thereof shall be borne equally by Buyer and Seller.

7. *Indemnification:*

Seller shall hold Buyer free and harmless from all unpaid or outstanding accounts payable, accrued expenses, salaries, wages, rent, and payroll, sales, and business taxes incurred or accruing prior to the close of escrow. All such obligations shall remain with and are chargeable to Seller.

8. *Regulatory Agencies:*

Seller shall obtain clearance from the State Board of Equalization and the Department of Benefit Payments stating that there is no further tax due. If any tax is due, Seller shall pay said tax prior to close of escrow. All social security, withholding, sales, and unemployment insurances taxes to the city, state, and federal government shall be paid or provided for by Seller up to the date of closing.

9. *Inventory, Bill of Sale, and Security Agreement:*

Seller shall deliver to Buyer through escrow, at the close thereof, an inventory and bill of sale covering furniture, fixtures, and leasehold improvements being purchased hereby. Buyer agrees that Seller may effect a security interest in its favor in the assets listed in the inventory by a UCC-1 filing. Subject only to such security interests in favor of Seller, all assets, including furniture, fixtures, and equipment, shall be transferred to Buyer free and clear. Seller shall pay all current liabilities incurred prior to _____, through escrow including any outstanding balances on equipment or fixtures. Prior to the close of escrow, a UCC-3 search shall be conducted to disclose any security interests encumbering the assets being purchased. All such encumbrances shall be paid by Seller and all such interests released prior to the close of escrow.

10. *Escrow Instructions:*

The parties acknowledge that Escrow Number ___ at _____ Escrow Corporation has been opened to consummate this transaction. The amendment shall constitute instructions and authorization to escrow holder to allocate the purchase price and perform a UCC-3 search.

11. *Assignment of Lease:*

This agreement of sale is subject to assignment of the lease from Seller to Buyer.

12. *Default:*

Buyer agrees to pay the rent and perform all terms and provisions of the existing lease covering the business premises and agrees that a default in Buyer's performance under said lease shall constitute a breach of this agreement and shall be subject to all legal and equitable remedies available to Seller in addition to those set forth in this agreement or elsewhere.

*   *   *

SELLER:

Dated: _____   _____

_____

BUYER:

Dated: _____   _____

_____

Appendix G

List of Relevant IRS Publications and Order Blank

The publications listed below are free. I have culled them from a larger list in order to present you with the IRS publications that you might want to review in connection with the concepts discussed in this book. You can use the order blank that follows to send for these publications or for any tax forms, schedules, or instructions you might need.

Number	Publication Description
523	Tax Information on Selling Your Home
530	Tax Information for Owners of Homes, Condominiums, and Cooperative Apartments
534	Depreciation
535	Business Expenses
536	Net Operating Losses and the At-Risk Limits
537	Installment Sales
541	Tax Information on Partnerships
542	Tax Information on Corporations
544	Sales and Other Dispositions of Assets
545	Interest Expense
550	Investment Income and Expenses

How to Get IRS Forms and Publications

You can order federal tax forms and publications from the IRS Forms Distribution Center for your state at the address below. Use the order blank at the bottom of this page. Or, if you prefer, you can photocopy tax forms from reproducible copies kept at many participating public libraries. In addition, many of these libraries have reference sets of IRS publications which you can also read or copy—on the spot.

Alabama—Caller No. 848, Atlanta, GA 30370

Alaska—P.O. Box 12626, Fresno, CA 93778

Arizona—P.O. Box 12626, Fresno, CA 93778

Arkansas—P.O. Box 2924, Austin, TX 78769

California—P.O. Box 12626, Fresno, CA 93778

Colorado—P.O. Box 2924, Austin, TX 78769

Connecticut—P.O. Box 1040, Methuen, MA 01844

Delaware—P.O. Box 25866, Richmond, VA 23260

District of Columbia—P.O. Box 25866, Richmond, VA 23260

Florida—Caller No. 848, Atlanta, GA 30370

Georgia—Caller No. 848, Atlanta, GA 30370

Hawaii—P.O. Box 12626, Fresno, CA 93778

Idaho—P.O. Box 12626, Fresno, CA 93778

Illinois—P.O. Box 338, Kansas City, MO 64141

Indiana—P.O. Box 6900, Florence, KY 41042

Iowa—P.O. Box 338, Kansas City, MO 64141

Kansas—P.O. Box 2924, Austin, TX 78769

Kentucky—P.O. Box 6900, Florence, KY 41042

Louisiana—P.O. Box 2924, Austin, TX 78769

Maine—P.O. Box 1040, Methuen, MA 01844

Maryland—P.O. Box 25866, Richmond, VA 23260

Massachusetts—P.O. Box 1040, Methuen, MA 01844

Michigan—P.O. Box 6900, Florence, KY 41042

Minnesota—P.O. Box 338, Kansas City, MO 64141

Mississippi—Caller No. 848, Atlanta, GA 30370

Missouri—P.O. Box 338, Kansas City, MO 64141

Montana—P.O. Box 12626, Fresno, CA 93778

Nebraska—P.O. Box 338, Kansas City, MO 64141

Nevada—P.O. Box 12626, Fresno, CA 93778

New Hampshire—P.O. Box 1040, Methuen, MA 01844

New Jersey—P.O. Box 25866, Richmond, VA 23260

New Mexico—P.O. Box 2924, Austin, TX 78769

New York—

　Western New York: P.O. Box 260, Buffalo, NY 14201

　Eastern New York (including New York City): P.O. Box 1040, Methuen, MA 01844

North Carolina—Caller No. 848, Atlanta, GA 30370

North Dakota—P.O. Box 338, Kansas City, MO 64141

Ohio—P.O. Box 6900, Florence, KY 41042

Oklahoma—P.O. Box 2924, Austin, TX 78769

Oregon—P.O. Box 12626, Fresno, CA 93778

Pennsylvania—P.O. Box 25866, Richmond, VA 23260

Rhode Island—P.O. Box 1040, Methuen, MA 01844

South Carolina—Caller No. 848, Atlanta, GA 30370

South Dakota—P.O. Box 338, Kansas City, MO 64141

Tennessee—Caller No. 848, Atlanta, GA 30370

Texas—P.O. Box 2924, Austin, TX 78769

Utah—P.O. Box 12626, Fresno, CA 93778

Vermont—P.O. Box 1040, Methuen, MA 01844

Virginia—P.O. Box 25866, Richmond, VA 23260

Washington—P.O. Box 12626, Fresno, CA 93778

West Virginia—P.O. Box 6900, Florence, KY 41042

Wisconsin—P.O. Box 338, Kansas City, MO 64141

Wyoming—P.O. Box 2924, Austin, TX 78769

Foreign Addresses—Taxpayers with mailing addresses in foreign countries should send their requests for forms and publications to: IRS Distribution Center, P.O. Box 25866, Richmond, VA 23260.

Puerto Rico—Director's Representative, U.S. Internal Revenue Service, Federal Office Building, Chardon Street, Hato Rey, PR 00918

Virgin Islands—Department of Finance, Tax Division, Charlotte Amalie, St. Thomas, VI 00801

Detach At This Line

Please follow these guidelines when ordering IRS forms and publications. This will help us process your order as quickly as possible. You will receive two copies of each form or schedule you request and one copy of each publication or instruction booklet. Please order only the items you need.

FORMS/INSTRUCTIONS/SCHEDULES

- In the box to the left, list each form, instruction booklet, and schedule you need *by its number, not its title*. List forms and instructions in numerical order. List schedules in alphabetical order. (When ordering instructions or schedules, be sure to identify the forms they go with.)
- In the box to the right, list each publication you need *by its number, not its title*. Please list them in numerical order.
- Carefully print or type your name and address on the label provided below. This label will be used to send your order to you.
- Detach above and mail this order form and label to the IRS address shown for your area.

PUBLICATIONS

Internal Revenue Service

| Name |
| Number and street |
| City or town, State, and ZIP code |

Appendix H
Abbreviations

AFTR	American Federal Tax Reports, First Series
aq'd	Acquiesced
CCH	Commerce Clearing House, Inc.
ERTA	Economic Recovery Tax Act of 1981
F.2d	Federal Reporter, Second Series
F. Supp.	Federal Supplement
IRC	Internal Revenue Code
IRS	Internal Revenue Service
ITC	Investment Tax Credit
non-acq.	Non-acquiescence
P-H	Prentice-Hall, Inc.
TC	Tax Court
TCM	Tax Court Memorandum Decisions
TEFRA	Tax Equity and Fiscal Responsibility Act of 1982
TRA	Tax Reform Act
U.S.	United States Reports
USC	United States Code
USCA	United States Code Annotated
USTC	United States Tax Cases

REFERENCES

Anderson, Paul E., *Tax Factors in Real Estate Operations,* 4th ed. (Englewood Cliffs, N.J.: Prentice-Hall, 1976).

Clurman, David, and Hebard, Edna L., *Condominiums and Cooperatives* (New York: John Wiley & Sons, 1970).

Faggen, Ivan, Blockowicz, David J., Schwieters, John T., Bradford, Dallas H., Brown, John B., Schwarz, Michael, Stevens, Jr., R. H., Waters, Duance, E., *Federal Taxes Affecting Real Estate,* 5th ed. (New York: Matthew Bender, 1984).

Greer, Gaylon E., *The Real Estate Investor and the Federal Income Tax,* rev. ed. (New York: John Wiley & Sons, 1978).

Kellog, Irving, *How to Use Financial Statements,* 2d ed. (Colorado Springs, Colorado: Shepard's/McGraw-Hill, 1979).

O'Bryne, John C., and Davenport, Charles, *Farm Income Tax Manual,* 6th ed. (Indianapolis, Indiana: The Allen Smith Company, 1982).

Index

ABOUT THE AUTHOR

Nelson E. Brestoff practices law in the Woodland Hills suburb of Los Angeles, California. He graduated from UCLA in 1971 with a bachelor of science degree in systems engineering. He received his master of science degree in environmental engineering science in 1972 from the California Institute of Technology. In 1975 he graduated from the Law Center at the University of Southern California, where he was a member of the Law Review. After law school, Mr. Brestoff served as a deputy city attorney for the city of Los Angeles for two years and has, since then, been in private practice.

From 1979 to 1983, Mr. Brestoff served on the board of directors of the West Los Angeles Regional Chamber of Commerce.

Mr. Brestoff emphasizes real estate and business transactions and litigation in his practice and is involved in real estate syndication and development with his clients and partners.

Mr. Brestoff's first book, *How to Borrow Money Below Prime*, was published by Simon and Schuster in 1985. His writing has also appeared in the *Los Angeles Times*, the *University of Southern California Law Review*, and the *Town Hall Reporter*.

ABOUT SAMUEL K. FRESHMAN

Samuel K. Freshman is of counsel to the law firm he helped to found: Freshman, Marantz, Orlanski, Comsky & Deutsch, of Beverly Hills, California. A graduate of Stanford University and Stanford Law School, he is a general partner in numerous real estate partnerships. As a member of the California Real Estate Commissioner's and California Corporations Commissioner's Advisory Committee, he assisted in drafting California's syndication regulations. Mr. Freshman has served as chairman of the Legal Committee of the California Association of Realtors, Syndication Division; national secretary of the Real Estate Securities Institute; chairman of the Real Property Division of the Beverly Hills Bar Association; and vice-chairman of the American Bar Association Real Property Section Committee on Trade Associations and Real Estate Investment Trusts.

He is a former adjunct professor of Real Estate Law, Graduate School of Business, University of Southern California.

During Mr. Freshman's career, he has been chairman of the board of both a commercial bank and a title insurance company, and has held directorships in several other large commercial enterprises.